Macmillan
Series Edit
   Eme

Advanced E
Advanced V
Applied Val
Asset Valu
Building Ec
Building Mc
Building Mc
Building Pro
Building Pro
Building Qu
Building Sur
Building Te
Civil Engine
   Ivor H.
Civil Engine
Commercia
Computers
Conflicts in
Constructa
   Tony Si
Constructio
Constructio
Contract Pl
   B. Cook
Contract Pl
Cost Estim
Design-Bui
Developme
Environme
Environme
European
Facilities M
Greener Buildings – Environmental impact of Property   Stuart J.
Housing Associations Helen Cope
Housing Management: Changing Practice Christine Davies (e
Information and Technology Applications in Commercial Proper
   Rosemary Feenan and Tim Dixon (editors)
Introduction to Building Services, second edition Christopher A. Howard
   and Eric C. Curd
Introduction to Valuation, third edition David Richmond
Marketing and Property People Owen Bevan
Principles of Property Investment and Pricing, second edition
   W. D. Fraser
Project Management and Control D. W. J. Day
Property Finance David Isaac
Property Valuation Techniques David Isaac and Terry Steley
Public Works Engineering Ivor H. Seeley

List continued overleaf

List *continued from previous page*

Quality Assurance in Building Alan Griffith
Quantity Surveying Practice Ivor H. Seeley
Recreation Planning and Development Neil Ravenscroft
Resource Management for Construction M. R. Canter
Small Building Works Management Alan Griffith
Structural Detailing, second edition P. Newton
Sub-Contracting under the JCT Standard Forms of Building Contract
    Jennie Price
Urban Land Economics and Public Policy, fifth edition
    P. N. Balchin, J. L. Kieve and G. H. Bull
Urban Renewal – Theory and Practice Chris Couch
1980 JCT Standard Form of Building Contract, second edition
    R. F. Fellows

Series Standing Order
If you would like to receive future titles in this series as they are published, you can
make use of our standing order facility. To place a standing order please contact your
bookseller or, in case of difficulty, write to us at the address below with your name
and address and the name of the series. Please state with which title you wish to
begin your standing order. (If you live outside the United Kingdom we may not have
the rights for your area, in which case we will forward your order to the publisher
concerned.)

Customer Services Department, Macmillan Distribution Ltd
Houndmills, Basingstoke, Hampshire RG21 2XS, England

Property Valuation Techniques

David Isaac and Terry Steley

School of Surveying, University of Greenwich

MACMILLAN

First published 1991 by
THE MACMILLAN PRESS LTD
Houndmills, Basingstoke, Hampshire RG21 2XS
and London
Companies and representatives
throughout the world

ISBN 0–333–56369–7 hardcover
ISBN 0–333–47151–2 paperback

A catalogue record for this book is available
from the British Library.

11   10   9   8   7   6   5   4   3
03   02   01   00   99   98   97   96   95

Printed in Hong Kong

For Daphne and Evelyn

Contents

Preface

This book is intended as an introduction to alternative approaches to real property valuation methods. It should be made clear at the beginning that we are talking about property appraisal which involves the initial valuation of property and subsequent analysis. The book outlines the traditional valuation and a critique of the approach, but does not dwell on this. Its aim is to extend considerations of alternative approaches to valuation and analysis of property investments.

The book will be useful for a number of different groups, including students, practitioners and also those whose background is not in the property field. For the student, it extends the basic texts and updates them to allow for developments in valuation techniques. It is thus an important book for those looking to develop valuation methods at the second and third year undergraduate level and also as a basis for postgraduate work. For the practitioner, the book is not intended to be too theoretical but to show applications of the different techniques in practice; as such, it is a useful reference book, and essential for the practitioner intending to keep abreast of developments in techniques. Finally, it is useful for professionals associated with property who may not be trained surveyors; this is because the book looks outwards from the property sector and tries to relate the techniques of property appraisal to those used in other sectors by other types of professional. The approach is based on practice and learning situations and, where possible, each chapter is made to be self-contained to aid reference, and thus there is some repetition of content; however, cross-references are included where a greater amount of background to any situation is required. The treatment is intended to parallel moves within the profession to take a less insular view of property appraisal and provide solutions which are acceptable and understandable to clients and professionals from other backgrounds; it aims to take the reader into new avenues of thought and discussion rather than down a route of more complex mathematical solutions, and looks to generate ideas about concepts rather than formulae. Where formulae are included, every effort has been made to simplify them and present them in a simple and usable way.

The book has a chapter on computer applications but does not just pay lip service to relating the appraisals to computer usage. The layout of the valuations and formulae, as well as adding clarity, in many cases provides a structure from which the reader can construct a spreadsheet calculation, and the layout assists in some detail as to its arrangement.

Finally, the book aims to link the reader more readily to other areas of financial analysis. It opens up for the reader the wider role of investment and business, and provides comparisons with other business investments. This approach is important for a number of reasons: property valuation and analysis is not the exclusive domain of property valuation professionals but is shared with other surveyors, other professions involved in investment and asset management and investors, developers, landholders and corporate clients with property assets. The book aims to demystify the techniques and make them usable, in order to develop the concepts and practice of appraising property assets.

Chapter 1 is an introduction and serves as a critique of the traditional approaches to property valuation, while chapter 2 is important as an explanation of the traditional method. Readers conversant with the traditional method may choose to miss out chapter 2; conversely, those readers who may find the concepts in chapter 1 difficult initially should refer first to chapter 2.

We would like to thank Professor Ivor Seeley, the Series Editor, for his helpful advice in the preparation of this book; also Professor David Wills and staff at the School of Surveying, Thames Polytechnic for their help and support.

Thames Polytechnic   David Isaac
School of Surveying   Terry Steley
December 1990

ACKNOWLEDGEMENTS

The authors and publishers wish to thank the following for permission to use copyright material:

Financial Times for extracts from *Financial Times*, 10th July, 1990.

Every effort has been made to trace all the copyright holders, but if any have been inadvertently overlooked the publishers will be pleased to make the necessary arrangement at the first opportunity.

1 Introduction

There is a need for alternative approaches to traditional valuation methods. This has arisen for several reasons. In the first place, large-scale investment in the property sector in recent years has led to more monitoring of investment situations and comparison of the price paid for investments with their eventual performance. Secondly, decreasing returns in the sector have led investors, especially institutional investors, to reappraise their investments and the investment criteria. Thirdly, there is a mood abroad of public awareness akin to consumerism, and this has expressed itself in more attention being paid to the activities of property professionals with specialists in other areas trying to come to terms with the level of property values and attempting to clarify property valuation methods used. Finally, there is in general more attention being paid to analysis of property transactions and performance from investment analysts, such as stockbrokers and analysts, trying to appraise property investments.

The property crash in the early 1970s focused attention on the valuation methods used in the profession and the debate has continued since then. Several writers including Baum and Crosby (1988) have discussed the basic need to distinguish between property valuation for purchase and subsequent analysis of performance (subsequent to purchase). We have tried to conform with the developments of these ideas, and in this book we deal generally with property appraisal which covers the valuation of property investments (that is, the calculation of the exchange value of a property) and with the subsequent analysis of the performance of the investment being the appraisal of its actual worth. It is appreciated that calculations before and after purchase will not agree precisely, because of the lack of perfect knowledge in the market at the time of the transaction and the inability to assess future changes in circumstances accurately. Problems of inefficiencies in the market are discussed later in this chapter, but it is sufficient to note that in most circumstances we will be dealing with property valuation, although the techniques can be used for subsequent analysis. The types of techniques in this book suggest improvements in existing approaches to property valuation and analysis. Other techniques introduce new concepts compared with traditional methods. To begin, we need to compare and contrast traditional methods, and analyse the criticisms of them.

1

THE TRADITIONAL METHOD

The traditional method achieves a present value for a property investment
by capitalising the cash flow arising from the investment over the life of the
asset. The traditional method is dealt with in more detail in chapter 2, but
it is interesting to consider the traditional method as a form of discounted
cash flow which has become more complex and perhaps corrupted as it has
developed more sophisticated and perhaps less understandable techniques.
The basis of the traditional calculation is the summation of the cash flows
over the life of the asset, these flows being discounted back to present
values. In its simplest form, in a freehold calculation the cash flows are
assumed to go on to infinity and if the property is let at the full rental value
(the full open market rental value), the cash flow remains unchanged from
the first year. The cash flows are then discounted back at an appropriate
yield, commonly called the 'all risks yield'. The reader should note that the
yield here relates to a situation where the property is already let at full
market value and not at a rent which is below this. This latter case would
be a term and reversion situation, where a rent below the existing market
rent would be revised at the next review-opportunity to full market value.
Note that, in the traditional analysis, we are always dealing with present-
day rents and not making assumptions of changes in the future. Even in a
term and reversion situation, the full rental value at the rent review date is
assessed on today's standard. So, the first important point to note about
the traditional method of property valuation is that it deals with static cash
flows which will only be revised to bring the rent to the full rental value
when the rent has been suppressed by the terms and conditions agreed for
the lease of the property. Variations in the cash flow which may happen in
the future are taken into account in the yield used. This we have called the
'all risks yield' because it is set at a particular rate to allow implicitly for
changes in risk, inflation and other circumstances which may affect the
nature of the investment in the future. The problems relating to the
make-up of interest rates, and thus discount rates, are discussed in chapter
4.

To summarise, the traditional method involves the capitalisation of
rental values over the life of the asset; certain allowances have to be made
in some circumstances to ensure that the income is free of all outgoings,
but basically the income is capitalised to achieve a capital value at the
present time. In the case of a property let at the full rental value, the flows
of rent into the future are each discounted back at the same rate to a
present value and these present values are added together. Note that not
only are the cash flows static in the analysis but also the level of discount
applied to each cash flow is static, suggesting they are all of equal risk. In
the traditional approach, the calculation can be completed by using tables
of discount rates or by using the equation that underlies the tables directly.

The tables used generally are *Parry's Valuation Tables* and the table used in *Parry's* for this capitalisation process is the Year's Purchase table. The Year's Purchase table is more specifically known as the Present Value of £1 per annum table. This table, as suggested above, will discount a future income stream at the required yield to provide a present value. It is based on the use of a form of compound interest formulation which used in reverse will discount the future annual rental flows to a present capital value.

In case the reader is unfamiliar with the concept of discount, the approach can be explained in that £1 in one year's time is not worth as much as £1 now in general terms. (It could be, if the currency were revalued or there were to be negative inflation.) This is because of three factors. Firstly, if you have the £1 now you could use it for immediate consumption, so you have the benefit of consumption or the use of the goods bought for a year. Alternatively, you may not consume the £1 but use it as an investment for which you may get a further return in respect of interest or profit from an enterprise. The second reason for the £1 being worth more now is that there may be inflation over the period. Inflation will reduce the purchasing power of the £1, so although you will still receive £1, the real value will have fallen. The concept of real and money returns, and the difference between the two, are important areas of interest which are discussed later in this book. The third reason for £1 in a year's time being less valuable than £1 now is related to risk; the longer you wait for your money, then there is less likelihood that you will actually collect it because over the year there might be changes in circumstances which could mean that some or all of the £1 is lost. So it is better to have £1 in your pocket now than in a year's time. Note from this that the discounting factor works opposite to that of the interest on money invested. Interest will increase the present capital values over the time period to an increased capital value in the future; discounting will reduce this future capital sum over the period to a lesser capital sum now. The concepts of discounting and compounding interest are basic to all financial transactions and have been around since compound interest was rediscovered by Italian traders in the Middle Ages. It was said that the Ancient Greeks had methods of compounding interest, but relics of their bank statements have not survived the passage of time and it is difficult to confirm this.

The traditional method is thus based, as most investment appraisal approaches are, on dealing with the passage of money over time and thus discounting relating to time is important. Some simple techniques such as payback techniques do not use discounting and these are discussed later in chapter 16, but essentially the point is that money in the future is worth less than now. The reader will probably have heard the old chestnut of the valuation lecturer asking the student whether he would prefer to receive a

£1 now or have one in a year's time. The student replied that he would prefer a £1 in the future. The lecturer was astonished and asked why? The student replied "I would only spend it if I had it now." Of course, times change and today's students on being asked this question are more likely to enquire "Are you buying or selling?" and refer rapidly to a City Futures broker on their portable telephone.

In order to capitalise the income flow by the traditional method, let us look at example 1.1.

Example 1.1

An investment provides an income of £100 p.a. for two years. What is the present value if we discount the income flows at 10%?

Using *Parry's Tables:*

Income	£100
Year's purchase for 2 years at 10%	1.7355
Present value	£173.55

Alternatively, using a simplified discounted cash flow:

Cash flow:

year 1: Present Value of £100 in 1 year discounted @10%	=	£90.90
year 2: Present Value of £100 in 2 years discounted @10%	=	£82.64
	Total Present Value	£173.54

In this calculation, the cash flows are discounted back over the 1 or 2 year period at the 10% interest rate. The formula for discounting can be worked out, or the tables for the present values can be found in *Parry's Tables*. As we have seen, the discounting process is opposite to that for the compounding of interest, and thus in this case as we are discounting a particular sum back to the present, it is the reverse of adding interest to the capital sum. (There are a number of variations to this theme which are discussed later in the chapter.) The formula for compounding interest is

$$(1 + i)^n$$

where i is the interest rate as a decimal, and n is the number of years the interest accumulates. Thus for a present capital sum of £1, this equation will give a future capital value after n years at 10%. By raising to the power of n, interest on interest is added year by year. If, as we have said, discount is the opposite of this process, then the formula for discount is the inverse of that for interest:

$$\frac{1}{(1 + i)^n}$$

Thus the cash flow for year 1 is

$$£100 \times \frac{1}{(1 + 0.1)^1} = £90.90$$

and the cash flow for year 2 is

$$£100 \times \frac{1}{(1 + 0.1)^2} = £82.64$$

ALTERNATIVE APPROACHES

A number of criticisms have been levelled at traditional methods of valuation. In this section we look at those criticisms in detail and try to suggest possible solutions. In particular, where a major conceptual change is necessary, the reader is referred to other sections of the book.

Criticisms of the traditional methods would include:

1. *Changes in the timing of rent payments*
   The Year's Purchase needs to be adjusted for payments in advance rather than in arrears. Under modern leases, payments are made in advance not in arrears. *Parry's Tables* now include tables for payments made quarterly in advance. This is discussed further in chapter 9.

2. *Taxation*
   The effect of taxation on the income received is not taken into account in traditional valuations, and there are arguments to suggest that it should be. Taxation considerations could be important for short leaseholds. This is discussed further in chapter 10.

3. *Valuation of freehold interests*
   There are a number of criticisms of traditional methods in dealing with the valuation of freehold interests; these concentrate on the inability of the methods to deal with particular problems, for instance, growth in rental value, inflation, varying incomes and reversions. In this book

some suggestions are made as to the possible alternative approaches, the use of equated yields to deal with growth and inflation, the use of the hardcore method in situations of varying incomes, and the use of equivalent yields for reversions. Alternative approaches are introduced in chapters 5, 6 and 7.

4. *Valuation of leasehold interests*
   This is an area fraught with difficulties when leasehold valuations are carried out in the traditional method; some alternatives are complex, not easily understood and are variations on the traditional method which attempt to get to a so-called 'correct' analysis without dealing with the logic of the underlying concepts. Problems which have been noted here relate to the problem of capital recoupment in the leasehold valuation and, associated with this, the replacement of the original capital sum in money terms and real terms. There is a wide area of dispute relating to the use of the dual rate and the sinking fund. Detailed solutions of all the problems of traditional methods are not attempted here – the text concentrates on dealing with the major conceptual problems. Chapter 12 does attempt to deal with some leasehold difficulties.

The problems of the traditional approach and the possible solutions are outlined below.

THE TRADITIONAL APPROACH: CRITICISMS AND SOLUTIONS

Criticisms	*Solutions*
Rent in advance? ⟶	Use different tables (these are now incorporated in *Parry's Tables*)
Tax? ⟶	Net of tax valuation
Freehold valuations	
Growth? Inflation? ⟶	Discounted Cash Flow
⟶	Equated yields
Varying incomes ⟶	Hardcore method
⟶	Equivalent yields

Leasehold valuations

Annual Sinking Fund (ASF)?
Level of ASF?
Tax on ASF?
Varying profit rents? —————————→ Double sinking fund
method etc.

We shall now consider some of these areas in more detail.

Rent Payments

The conventional approach assumes that the rent is paid and is received annually in arrears. In practice, rents are usually paid in advance, usually quarterly in advance. The effect of this does not require a change in the valuation approach but just sets of different tables, such as *Bowcock's* or *Rose's*, and also the quarterly in advance tables now in *Parry's Tables*. The change from payment in arrears to in advance will increase the Year's Purchase, so that if the capital value of the investment is to be the same as that previously valued using payments in arrear, one will need to use a higher yield and thus a lower Year's Purchase (YP) in the calculation.

The relationship between the YP single rate in arrears and in advance can be shown as follows:

YP in advance (*n* periods) = YP in arrears (*n* − 1 periods) + 1

For example, for annual rents:

YP in advance for 10 years @ 10% = (YP in arrears for 9 years @ 10%) + 1
6.759 = 5.759 + 1

and for quarterly rents:

YP in advance for 40 quarters @ 2.4% = (YP in arrears for 39 quarters
@ 2.4%) + 1
26.15 = 25.15 + 1

Note that the tables will provide the multiplier for the relevant number of periods, which can be any length (quarterly, annually etc.) but one must ensure that the interest rate is consistent with the period used. In this case, 2.4% is used as the quarterly rate which when compounded will provide an annual rate of 10%. This is shown as follows: on an annual basis, £1 will compound to £1.10 at an interest rate of 10% over one year. Using the formula for the amount of £1 (the amount £1 will grow to over one year at 10% p.a., also known as compound interest), $(1 + i)^n$, then £1 becomes $£(1 + 0.10)^1$ where i is 0.10 as a decimal and n is 1 year. On a quarterly basis, the same answer will be provided by $n = 4$ and $i = 0.024$, thus $(1 + 0.024)^4 = 1.10$.

So to find the quarterly interest rate:

$$(1 + 0.10)^1 = (1 + x)^4$$

and solving for x:

$$x = (1.1)^{\frac{1}{4}} - 1$$

Taxation

The usual approach taken in traditional valuations is that the valuation is completed gross of tax, because the tax payable depends on the status of the recipient and this might not always be known. In the market, of course, there are a number of different players with differing tax considerations. It is possible to use the conventional method on a true net approach:

Gross valuation	
FRV	£10,000
YP @ 10% gross	10
Capital value	£100,000
True net valuation	
FRV	£10,000
less tax @ 40%	£4,000
True net income	£6,000
YP @ 6% net	16.67
Capital value	£100,000

The net rate used in the net-of-tax calculation is the gross rate less the tax on that rate – that is, 10% less 4% (40% of 10%); the net rate is generally the gross rate $\times$ 1 − t. In order to gross-up a net rate to the gross rate then we can multiply by $[1/(1−t)]$. Chapter 10 looks in more detail at net-of-tax valuations.

Leasehold Valuations

The criticisms of leasehold valuations concentrate on two areas: firstly the problems of capital recoupment and secondly errors in the valuations occurring with varying profit rentals. These are discussed below, but it should be mentioned that the traditional method in adjusting the freehold yield and then making allowance for a sinking fund is trying to compare the leasehold with the freehold interest. It might well be that, especially for short leaseholds, such an approach is fundamentally flawed and that the yields associated should be drawn from comparable investments outside the property sector based on the life of the asset and the risk associated with the cash flows arising. This latter point should be borne in mind when considering the detailed criticisms outlined below.

(a) Problems of capital recoupment

(i) Replacement of capital. The sinking fund is used to put the leasehold and freehold interests on equal footings so that the appropriate yield structure can be determined. The concept of capital recoupment is that the asset does not depreciate but is renewed at the end of its life by the purchase of an identical investment. As indicated above, this approach is tenuous – for instance, will such an identical investment be available?

(ii) The annual sinking fund does not allow for inflation. The traditional approach allows for a sinking fund to replace the original cost of the asset. Even allowing for inflation without additional growth or changes in the levels of value, this would not provide sufficient funds to replace the asset in a period of inflation, as has been experienced since the late 1950s in the UK. The annual sinking fund (ASF) replaces the original capital only, but it may be possible to use the ASF to replace a greater capital sum than the original outlay by inflating that sum using the Amount of £1 table and an appropriate inflation rate for the investment involved. If an inflated ASF is used, then the investment is as secure as the corresponding freehold (in theory, if you have chosen the appropriate inflation rate); this would mean that the leasehold rate applied in these circumstances would be at a lower yield, but the higher sinking fund would offset this and a lower YP would be produced, in turn reducing the capital value compared with the traditional approach. It is also possible that the lease may appreciate in the short term if there is sufficient time before expiry, thus lessening the problem.

(iii) The annual sinking fund rate at $2\frac{1}{2}\%$ is unrealistic. The argument here is that the level of $2\frac{1}{2}\%$ is unrealistic because it is possible for investors to

earn more than this yield, and it is also unrealistic in the sense that most leaseholders do not make such a provision. It is important in this argument that the concept of trying to compare freeholds with leaseholds as outlined above is understood. Is it also important that provision is actually made if such an allowance has been assumed in the valuation; the approach has to be as coherent as possible and, without this allowance, what justification could there be to pin the yield on the freehold? The level of sinking fund could, of course, be adjusted but essentially it is intended as a notional allowance to adopt the yield structure. The rate of sinking fund used is likely to be low to reflect that the rate is guaranteed no matter what happens to interest rates and guarantees repayment at that rate. The rate is also net of tax. While the latter points cannot fully justify the level of rate used, it should be appreciated that the problems with leasehold valuations are of a more fundamental nature than the mere level of the sinking fund rate.

To counter the arguments above, suggestions have been made that the leasehold should be valued with an appropriate single rate or by using discounted cash flow methods; the rate used would accord with the yield on an appropriate comparable investment with an equivalent life, as suggested above.

(b) Problems of errors in valuing varying profit rentals

If profit rentals vary over the life of the leasehold asset there will be a tendency for errors in the valuation; because the sinking funds accumulating in each profit rent flow will not replace the asset, they undercompensate. This is a technical problem, and if this approach is used it will need to be corrected by one of the methods devised – for instance, the double sinking fund method. In using even more technical methods, you need to ensure that the rest of the market place is taken into account in your choice of comparable evidence!

Freehold Valuations

The criticisms of the use of the traditional investment method in valuing freehold interests relate to three areas:

* The use of an all risks yield
* Allowance for inflation, growth and different rent review patterns
* The valuation of varying incomes in terms and reversions.

The main solutions to these problems are discussed in this book. In the case of the all risks yield, the yield is analysed for the elements of inflation/growth, time preference and risk. To allow for inflation, growth and different rent review patterns, concepts of equated yields and constant rents are introduced, including the use of *Donaldson's* and *Rose's Tables*. For term and reversion, the hardcore method is discussed and the equivalent yield explored. Most of these solutions have their base in discounted cash flow (DCF) approaches.

Distinguishing Appraisal Valuation and Analysis

It is important at an early stage to clarify what is meant by 'valuation'. Baum and Crosby (1988), in their book *Property Investment Appraisal*, distinguish clearly between 'property appraisal' as a general term and the more specific terms of 'valuation' and 'analysis'. *Valuation* relates to the estimate of the price of a property for sale, while *analysis* is carried out after purchase to assess the correctness of the price initially paid. *Appraisal* covers both aspects. The concept of dealing with the ante and post purchase situation is an important one, and is mirrored in the adoption of alternative methods of appraisal. Once this important point is understood, the distinctions between best estimates and the resultant actual situation becomes clear. In this book, we will tend to use 'valuation' in its general accepted sense and only clarify it when the distinction becomes important. From the previously mentioned distinction it is obvious that the ante purchase situation may suit the implicit all risks yield approach because of the difficulties in estimating cash flows, whereas in analysis where cash flows are specific and known, an explicit DCF model could be used.

The difference between valuation and analysis is an important one. In the first case, valuation is all about assessing the price of an investment while analysis is an estimate of the worth of the investment. The divergence of market value and investment worth is an indication of an inefficient market. In order to fix the price of a property, the Royal Institution of Chartered Surveyors provides *Asset Valuation Standards guidance notes*. These notes define the open market value as the best price at which an interest in a property might reasonably be expected to be sold by private treaty at the date of valuation assuming:

- a willing seller
- a reasonable period within which to negotiate the sale, taking into account the nature of the property and the state of the market
- that values will remain static throughout the period
- that the property will be freely exposed to the market, and no account is to be taken of an additional bid by a special purchaser.

An analysis, on the other hand, considers the value or worth to a particular purchaser after taking account of his individual circumstances, his investment portfolio and possibly different assumptions about the future. So the analysis or estimate of investment worth is not necessarily market based, it is based on individual investors and reflects their subjective estimates of relevant factors. Worth could be a price or a rate of return.

Thus Property Appraisal is made up of:

- *Valuation* — the prediction of the most likely market price
- *Analysis* — the estimation of investment worth.

The Efficiency of the Property Market

The valuation process is not separated from the players in the market, as they tend to fix the price. The people who value property in the market are the same people who then negotiate the purchase and sale of properties and fix the price. If the one affects the other, then tests of valuation accuracy are irrelevant because the valuer will determine the price.

The operation of the market in property and the price paid can only be justified if the market is efficient — that is, if the market prices fully reflect the effects of decisions made in the market. An efficient market requires that dealing costs are not too high, relevant information about the investments is available to a largish number of participants, and no individual dominates the market. If individuals disagree on judgements as to the future returns of an investment then there will be transactions, and the sum of the transactions will provide an unbiased valuation in an efficient market. Such a market is described as a 'fair game' one. If the market is fair game, then *ex-post* gains or losses cannot be predicted *ex-ante*. The efficient market hypothesis analyses the investment markets in three forms: the weak, semi-strong and strong forms. The weak form hypothesis is based on the assumption that if the market is efficient, present prices reflect all that can be known about the investments in the market including previous prices; thus prices follow a so-called 'random walk' unaffected by previous price movements. Gerald Brown (1988) suggests that research in the UK shows that the property market is efficient in the weak form level but it may be that with a restricted market, such as in the forced sale of properties, there exist opportunities to achieve a purchase price below the equilibrium market value of the property.

REFERENCES

Baum, A. and Crosby N. (1988). *Property Investment Appraisal*, Routledge and Kegan Paul, London.

Britton, W., Davis, K. and Johnson, T. (1990). *Modern Methods of Valuation*, Estates Gazette, London.

Brown, G. R. (1988). 'Portfolio Theory and Property Investment Analysis', in A. R. MacLeary and N. Nanthakumaran (eds), *Property Investment Theory*, Spon, London.

APPENDIX: THE BASIS OF THE TABLES USED IN THE TRADITIONAL METHOD

In order to understand the basis of the traditional method and the calculation of compounding and discounting factors in investment calculations, we need to consider the tables which underpin the appraisals. In dealing with investment situations, we are considering the purchase of an asset to generate an income stream over a period of time. Thus we are converting the value of an income stream in the future into a present capital sum. The basis of the traditional approaches, the tables used in *Parry's Tables*, is about the conversion of present and futures sums and the conversion of capital and income streams. The tables deal with the process of compounding and discounting; for instance, the Amount of £1 table will add compound interest to an initial sum to give a future capital sum. The six main options of conversion are:

- Capital to income and vice versa
- Present sums to future sums and vice versa
- The compounding of sums into the future, and discounting back to the present.

Summary of the Valuation Tables

Amount of £1

This table provides the amount £1 will accumulate to over n years at an interest rate of i% p.a. It thus compounds up from a present capital sum to a future capital sum. The approach is commonly known as compound interest and the formula is A (Amount of £1) $= (1 + i)^n$.

PV of £1

The present value of £1 gives the sum which needs to be invested at the interest rate i to accumulate to £1 in n years. i discounts a future capital sum to a present capital sum; it is the process of the Amount of £1 in reverse and the formula is $1/A$.

Amount of £1 p.a.

This is the amount to which £1 invested annually will accumulate to in n years. It is thus compounding a present income stream to a future capital sum and the formula is $(A - 1)/i$.

Annual sinking fund (ASF) to produce £1

This is the amount which needs to be invested annually to accumulate to £1 in n years at an interest rate $i\%$. It thus discounts back the future capital sum to a present income stream.

Annuity £1 will purchase

This is the income stream that will be generated over n years by an original investment of £1. The income produced will be consumed as part capital and part interest on capital. Assuming the rates of consumption are the same, a single rate approach gives an equation $i/(1 - PV)$. If the rates differ, then the formula $(i + s)$ needs to be used, where s is the annual sinking fund formula above at a different interest rate from i. Note that this is the way a mortgage is calculated: the Building Society provides the initial capital sum and expects repayments of equal amounts throughout the loan period (assuming fixed rate money), but the repayments consist of interest and capital (that is, the sinking fund).

PV of £1 p.a.

The present value of £1 p.a. is the present value of the right to receive £1 p.a. over n years. The future income stream is discounted back to the present value and is the opposite of the annuity calculation. Thus the formulation for a single rate is $(1-PV)/i$ or for the dual rate, $1/(i+s)$, where s is the annual sinking fund at the sinking fund rate. This approach is commonly known as the Year's Purchase and gives the present value of a future stream of rental income.

Summary Table

Option	Cash flow		Formula
	Now	*Future*	
Amount of £1 (A)	Capital sum $\xrightarrow{\text{compounding}}$	Capital Sum	$A = (1 + i)^n$
PV of £1 (PV)	Capital sum $\xleftarrow{\text{discounting}}$	Capital Sum	$PV = \dfrac{1}{A}$
Amount of £1 p.a.	Income $\xrightarrow{\text{compounding}}$	Capital Sum	$\dfrac{A - 1}{i}$
ASF to produce £1 (ASF)	Income $\xleftarrow{\text{discounting}}$	Capital Sum	$ASF = \dfrac{i}{A - 1}$
Annuity £1 will purchase	Capital sum $\xrightarrow{\text{compounding}}$	Income	$\dfrac{(1 - PV)}{i}$
PV of £1 p.a. (YP)	Capital sum $\xleftarrow{\text{discounting}}$	Income (single rate)	$YP = \dfrac{i}{(1 - PV)}$

General Tables referred to

Bowcock, P., *Property Valuation Tables*, Macmillan, London, 1978.

Davidson, A. W., *Parry's Valuation and Investment Tables*, Estates Gazette, London, 1990.

Marshall, P., *Donaldson's Investment Tables*, Donaldsons, 1989.

Rose, J. J., *Property Valuation Tables*, Freeland Press, Aldershot, 1979.

Rose, J. J., *Tables of the Constant Rent,* The Technical Press, Oxford, 1976.

2 Traditional Method of Investment Valuation

This chapter is primarily intended to introduce the problems associated with the traditional, or conventional, method of valuing investment properties which the techniques outlined in this book attempt to address. Because the text requires knowledge of valuation methods and there may be some readers who do not fully understand the basis of the investment method of valuations, this elementary outline is included – although study of an introductory valuations text such as *Introduction to Valuations* (Richmond, 1985) will be of considerable value to those readers not conversant with traditional valuation techniques.

Most investors seek to obtain a return on their invested money either as an annual income or a capital gain; the investment method of valuation is traditionally concerned with the former.

Where the investor has a known sum of money to invest on which a particular return is required, the income can be readily calculated from:

$$\text{Income} = \text{Capital} \times \frac{i}{100} \text{ where } i = \text{rate of return required}$$

For example, if £10,000 is to be invested with a required rate of return of 8%, the income will be:

$$\text{Income} = £10,000 \times \frac{8}{100} = £800$$

In this type of problem, the capital sum is known and the income is to be calculated. In the case of real property, the income (rent) is known, either from the actual rent passing under the lease or estimated from the letting of similar comparable properties, and the capital sum needs to be calculated. The formula above has to be changed so that capital becomes the subject:

$$\text{Capital} = \text{Income} \times \frac{100}{i}$$

Example 2.1

What capital sum should be paid for an investment producing £8,000 per annum where a return of 8% is required?

$$\text{Capital} = £800 \times \frac{100}{8} = £10,000$$

This process is known as 'capitalising' the income, that is, converting an annual income into a capital sum. It is essential that the income capitalised is 'net', that is, clear of any expenses incurred by the investment, so therefore the formula can be modified to:

$$C = NI \times \frac{100}{i} \quad \text{where} \quad \begin{array}{l} C = \text{capital} \\ NI = \text{net income} \\ i = \text{rate of return required} \end{array}$$

For given rates of return which extend to perpetuity, $100/i$ will be constant. For example:

Rate of return	100/i
10%	10
8%	12.5
12%	8.66

This constant is known as the Present Value of £1 per annum, or more commonly in real property valuation the Year's Purchase, abbreviated to *YP*. The formula can thus be finally modified to:

$$C = NI \times YP$$

The *YP* calculated by using $100/i$ will only apply to incomes received in perpetuity, which are limited to those received from freehold interests let at full market rent, or rack rent. For incomes to be received for shorter periods, the *YP* must be calculated using a different formula, but tables of constants are available. The most commonly used, particularly in the traditional method, are *Parry's Valuation and Conversion Tables*. Two essential elements required in the analysis are (a) the period of time the investment lasts, that is, the number of years, and (b) the rate of return required, usually known as the yield.

To estimate the value of an investment in real property, two elements are required:

1. the net income to be received
2. the required yield.

The first will be obtained from the lease of the subject property or, if the property is unlet, an estimate of rental value obtained from lettings of comparable properties, and the second from an analysis of sales of comparable investments. A valuer must therefore have a knowledge of two separate markets – the letting market and the investment market.

YIELD

The decision on what investments are to be made will depend on the personal preferences of the investor. However, there are five essential factors which will affect the decision. These are:

1. *Security of income.* This refers not only to the certainty and regularity of payment but also to security in 'real terms', that is the maintenance of its purchasing power. There must be frequent reviews of the rent paid under the lease and the prospect of 'growth' in rent must be good, at least in line with inflation.

2. *Security of capital.* As for rent, the value of the invested capital must not be reduced by the effect of inflation. As the capital value is directly related to income, it will be secured in real terms where there is acceptable growth in rent.

3. *Transfer costs.* Investors want to incur minimum costs in acquisition and disposal of their investments.

4. *Liquidity.* The investment must have the ability to convert rapidly into cash for re-investment elsewhere.

5. *Effect of taxation.* This will depend on the tax position of the investor.

The yield required from a particular investment will reflect the investor's view of the risks likely to be met. Where the risks are seen to be high, a high yield will be required as compensation. A low yield will be accepted where the risks are considered to be low. In the traditional method, a single yield is used and therefore it has become known as the 'all risks yield'. A simple example will illustrate its use.

Example 2.2

Estimate the value of the freehold interest in shop premises in a secondary location and let at a net rent of £8,000 per annum on a lease having 4 years remaining. The net rental value is estimated to be £15,000 per annum.

Valuation:
From analysis of comparable premises in secondary locations, a yield of 8% is considered appropriate.

Term	Net rent received £8,000	
	YP 4 yrs @ 7% 3.39	
		£27,120
Reversion	Net rental value £15,000	
	YP in perp. def. 4 yrs @8% 9.19	
		£137,850
		£164,970

Estimated capital value £165,000

Notes:

1. No attempt is made to quantify the level of rent in 4 year's time.
2. The rent will therefore remain unchanged in perpetuity.
3. Any potential growth in income is reflected in the all risks yield of 8%.
4. The income during the term is considered to be more secure because the lessee is enjoying a 'profit rent' of £7,000 (market rent £15,000 *less* rent payable of £8,000), and therefore is less likely to default in payment of rent, so the yield for this income is reduced. The amount of reduction is dependent on the subjective views of the valuer and can range from 0.5% to 1.5%. In this case, as the rental value is nearly twice the rent received, 1% is considered appropriate.

The leasehold interest would be considered to be a less attractive investment than the freehold, because the freeholder's consent is required for any proposed alteration to the property or disposal by assignment, or sub-letting. Also, it is common practice for lease terms to place responsibility for all repairs and reinstatement insurance on the leaseholder. For this reason, the leasehold yield used is found by adding 0.5–1% to the freehold yield. Furthermore, the leasehold interest is regarded as a wasting asset and therefore an annual sinking fund is established to replace the capital cost of the interest on expiry of the lease. Typically, the insurance policies used for sinking funds must be virtually 'riskless' and therefore have a low rate of interest, but this rate must be netted down to allow for the effect of tax paid on the income earned by the policy. As an annual sinking fund is not deductible for income tax purposes, the annual amount to be allowed must be grossed up by the rate of tax paid by the investor.

Example 2.3

The valuation of the leasehold interest in the above example would be:

Net rental value	£15,000	
Net rent paid	£8,000	
Profit rent	£7,000	
YP 4 yrs @ 9% & 3% (tax 40%)	2.05	
Estimated capital value		£14,350

Leasehold investments are therefore valued by using YP Dual Rate adjusted for Tax Tables; one rate is used for the yield, the other for the sinking fund, the latter rate being netted down and the required sum being grossed up to allow for the effect of income tax. The yield is based on an arbitrary adjustment of the freehold yield and not found from analysis of similar investments. In practice, annual sinking funds are very rarely used for leasehold investments because of the low interest rates. The tax rate used again is arbitrary unless valuing is being done for a particular investor whose tax rate is known.

Further consideration of leasehold valuation is made in chapter 12, and a detailed explanation of the tax adjustments is given in chapter 10.

OTHER CONCEPTS OF YIELD

Initially it would seem that on purchasing the investment, the investor will obtain an 8% return. But is this so?

$$\text{Return on capital} = \frac{\text{Income}}{\text{Capital}} \times 100\%$$

$$\frac{£8,000}{£165,000} \times 100 = 4.85\%$$

Obviously, this 'initial yield' is nothing like 8% nor the 7% used to capitalise the term rent. However, what has not been considered is the increase in capital value which occurs simply by the reversion coming a year closer, as the following shows:

Valuation in one year's time

Term	Net rent received	£8,000	
	YP 3 yrs @ 7%	2.62	
			£20,960

Reversion	Net rental value	£15,000	
	YP in perp. def. 3 yrs @ 8%	9.92	
			£148,800
			£169,760

Estimated capital value   £170,000

This shows an increase in capital value of £5,000 which if it is added to the income gives a notional total income of £13,000. The yield then becomes:

$$\frac{£13,000}{£165,000} \times 100 = 7.9\%$$

which is very close to the 8% all risks yield expected.

Where the property is let at full rental value, then the initial yield will be the same as the all risks yield. This can be seen by an examination of the leasehold interest. In this, the income is capitalised after allowing for the tax adjusted sinking fund.

	Profit rent		£7,000
Less	Annual sinking fund		
	Capital to be replaced	£14,350	
	ASF 4 yrs @ 3%	0.239	
	Annual sum payable	£3,430	
	Gross Tax factor @ 40%	1.667[*]	
	Total allowance for ASF		5,718
	Remaining income		£1,282

$$\text{Return on capital } \frac{\pounds1,282}{\pounds14,350} \times 100 = 9\%$$

The capital value of the freehold will continue to increase until reversion occurs. It will then be:

Net rental value	£15,000	
YP in perp. @ 8%	12.5	
Capital value		£187,500

The return on capital when reversion will be:

$$\frac{\pounds15,000}{\pounds165,000} \times 100 = 9.09\%$$

This is known as the 'reversionary yield', which is obviously higher than the all risks yield required, but no account has been taken of the £22,500 increase in capital value.

 Supposing rental values increase by 10% per annum, what will the reversionary yield be?

Present net rental value	£15,000	
Amount of £1 in 4 yrs @ 10%	1.46	
Rental Value in 4 years, say		£22,000

In which case the reversionary yield would then be:

$$\frac{\pounds22,000}{\pounds165,000} \times 100 = 13.33\%$$

The capital value will be:

Net rental value	£22,000	
YP in perp. @ 8%	12.5	
Capital value		£275,000

giving an increase in capital value of £110,000.

SUMMARY

The traditional method capitalises the net income by using a yield to reflect all the risks, including rental growth, as seen by the valuer, the yield being obtained from sales of comparable investments, frequently with no knowledge of the investment strategy of the purchaser. No specific consideration is given to the likelihood or magnitude of growth in rental values. Therefore a valuation using the conventional method gives very little information about the investment to a potential investor.

The concept of an all risks yield is too simplistic. There are several other concepts of yield of importance to an investor.

Leasehold interests are valued using a yield related to the freehold yield and not from analysis of sales of leasehold investments. Annual sinking funds are still provided for, though rarely used in practice.

REFERENCE

Richmond, D. (1985). *Introduction to Valuation*, 2nd edn, Macmillan.

3 Discounted Cash Flow

CASH FLOW

In recent times, the term 'cash flow' has been used in fairly common parlance – usually connected with a crisis – but managerial economists and analysts have used cash flow analysis in connection with business investments for many years. Stated simply, it can be considered as the total funds generated from operations – that is, the revenue received and the expenditure incurred, including initial cost, in an investment project; a project may be the purchase of a relatively small item of office equipment or a major property development scheme.

A cash flow appraisal would be based on:

1. The present and future costs, for instance, the acquisition cost of a machine and the on-going costs to keep the machine in production.
2. The future receipts generated, in this case the revenue from the output from the machine.
3. Value received, or cost incurred, on disposal of the asset.

Conventionally, incomes or revenues are regarded as positive amounts and expenditure regarded as negative amounts; therefore, if the cash flow analysis produces a positive result, a contribution to profit will be obtained, whereas a negative result indicates that a loss will be made.

Example 3.1

On considering the investment in an asset x to be purchased for £100 and which is estimated to produce £20 income per quarter for one year at the end of which the asset could be sold for £50, a simple cash flow statement would be:

Quarter	0	1	2	3	4
Income	0	20	20	20	20
Sale					50
Expenditure	−100				
Net income	−100	20	20	20	70
Cumulative balance	−100	−80	−60	−40	30

24

(Convention also usually shows base period as numbered 0 which is more convenient when using 'discounting', to be considered later.)

It can be seen that investment in asset *x* would show a net profit of £30 over outlay.

The reader will appreciate that this example is extremely simplistic; more detailed cash flows can be incorporated, such as allowance for interest to be paid on borrowing the initial cost, the effect of inflation, projected growth in income, tax liability and estimated depreciation of the asset.

Example 3.2

If the funding for asset *x* had to be borrowed at 5% rate of interest payable at the end of each quarter the analysis would be:

Quarter	0	1	2	3	4
Income	0	20	20	20	20
Sale					50
Expenditure: capital	−100				
interest		−5	−4.25	−3.46	−2.64
Net income	−100	15	15.75	16.54	67.36
Cumulative balance	−100	−85	−69.25	−52.71	14.65

The net profit has now been reduced to £14.65 by the total amount of interest paid of £15.35.

Cash flow analysis is helpful in decision-making with a single project, however more frequently a choice has to be made between alternatives. If the time basis is the same for the alternative, the simple cash flow basis shown above can be used to select which investment to make.

Example 3.3

Consider an alternative asset *y* costing £300 and generating £70 per quarter income with an end disposal value of £200. Using an interest rate of 5% the cash flow would look like:

Quarter	0	1	2	3	4
Income	0	70	70	70	70
Sale					200
Expenditure: capital	−300				
interest		−15	−12.25	−9.36	−6.33
Net income	−300	55	57.75	60.64	263.67
Cumulative balance	−300	−245	−187.25	−126.61	137.06

This shows a net contribution to profit of £137.06. It is not necessary to employ a highly skilled analyst to see that a return of £137.06 on £300 outlay is to be preferred to £14.65 on £100. Of course, the relative positions of the two investments will not alter when interest on borrowing is the same.

DISCOUNTED CASH FLOW

Comparison is not so simple when the alternatives being considered have varying costs and incomes generated over different periods of time. A technique used to overcome this difficulty is known as 'discounting', that is to bring all future amounts, revenue and expenditure, to present day values using a given rate of interest known as the 'discount rate'; by so doing, a cash flow becomes a 'Discounted Cash Flow' (DCF).

DCF is a technique developed by financial appraisers as a tool to assess the overall profitability of a project. Increasingly, the technique is being used by property valuers and analysts, very largely because as financial institutions became more involved in property development and investment they found the traditional approach of surveyors to be quite unacceptable. It copes with incomes and expenditures varying in amounts and in time periods (that is, yearly, monthly or for another period); in other words, the 'time value' of money is taken into consideration. It can also be used to compare capital projects, but there is some evidence to suggest that in practice simpler methods are used (such as payback).

As stated above, the technique is based on calculating the present worth of future sums of money, either income or expenditure, a technique not unknown to valuers who are familiar with using Present Value of £1 and Present Value of £1 per annum Tables from *Parry's*, which are the same as other tables published under the title 'DCF Tables'. Indeed it is sometimes argued that the traditional investment method estimates the present value of future periodic incomes and therefore 'DCF' is just jargon for what valuers have been doing for years. Figure 3.1 shows this diagrammatically

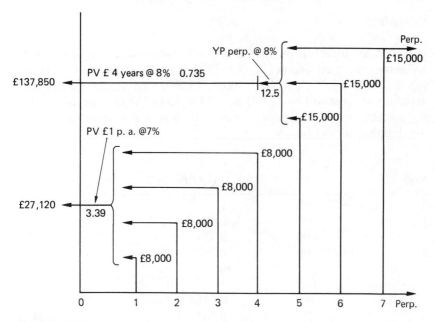

NPV £164,970

Figure 3.1

as applied to the simple freehold valuation in Example 2.2, chapter 2. It is true that the traditional method and DCF both find the net present value; however, the important difference lies in the thought processes involved in using the technique, particularly the rate of interest used.

To produce a DCF, the valuer has at least three forms of interest rate to choose from:

1. The rate which has to be paid for borrowing capital – the borrowing rate.
2. The rate which could be earned if the capital was invested elsewhere – the opportunity rate.
3. The rate of return which the investor requires to compensate for the risk involved, the loss of immediate consumption and inflation – the target rate.

In investment appraisal and analysis it is the target rate which is most commonly used. It could be related to Government stock rates.

Example 3.4

Consider an asset *A* purchased for £20,000 which will generate the
following estimated incomes: year 1, £3,000; year 2, £5,000; year 3, £6,000;
year 4, £3,000; year 5, £6,500; year 6, £5,750; year 7, £3,000. In year 4,
maintenance cost will be £1,000 and at the end of year 7 the asset will be
disposed of for £1,500. If a borrowing rate of 10% per annum is required,
the discounted cash flow will be:

Year		PV £1 @ 10%	DCF
0	−£20,000	1	−£20,000
1	3,000	0.909	2,727
2	5,000	0.826	4,130
3	6,000	0.751	4,506
4	3,000		
	−1,000	0.683	1,366
5	6,500	0.621	4,037
6	5,750	0.564	3,243
7	3,000		
	1,500	0.513	2,309
		Discounted cash flow	£2,318

The DCF is positive and thus the asset purchase is worthwhile. A cash flow
calculation would show a contribution to profit of £4,529, and this would
also indicate a worthwhile investment. Thus it can be seen that little is
gained by using a DCF approach when considering a single project,
however the technique can be invaluable when alternative investments are
to be compared.

Example 3.5

An alternative asset, *B*, will cost £21,750 but will produce the following
incomes: year 1, £2,500; year 2, £3,000; year 3, £4,750; year 5, £6,500; year
7, £4,500; year 8, £3,000. No maintenance costs will be incurred and there
will be no terminal value. Borrowing cost remains, of course, at 10%. The
DCF will be:

Year		PV £1 @ 10%	DCF
0	−£21,750	1	−£21,750
1	2,500	0.909	2,273
2	3,000	0.826	2,478
3	4,750	0.751	3,567
4	5,750	0.683	3,927
5	6,500	0.621	4,037
6	7,000	0.564	3,948
7	4,500	0.513	2,309
8	3,000	0.467	1,401
		Discounted cash flow	£2,189

A cash flow calculation would show a positive contribution to profits of £4,703, which is higher than the cash flow of investment *A*. Though the DCF also shows a positive contribution to profits, it is less than that of *A* which therefore would be the preferred investment. However the reason for this is because the bulk of the income is generated towards the end of asset *B*'s life, so other criteria might be used.

There are two forms of DCF used in investment analysis:

- Net Present Value (NPV)
- Internal Rate of Return (IRR)

Net Present Value (NPV)

This is the form of DCF demonstrated above, namely the result of discounting to the present day all sums of money, incoming and outgoing, which the investor incurs.

For single sums, the Present Value of £1 Table can be used, or it can be calculated by using the formula:

$$\frac{1}{(1 + i)^n}$$

This will be seen to be the inverse of the Amount of £1, or compound interest formula in Chapter 1.

Where the same amount is being received or spent for a series of years, then the Present Value of £1 per Annum can be used; this is more familiarly known as the Year's Purchase (YP). It can be seen that it is simply the sum of a series of individual Present Values. For example, using the rate of 8%:

PV £1 1 year @ 8%	0.9259
PV £1 2 years @ 8%	0.8573
PV £1 3 years @ 8%	0.7938
PV £1 4 years @ 8%	0.7350
YP 4 years @ 8%	3.3120

As stated above, the discount rate can be: (1) borrowing rate; (2) opportunity rate or (3) target rate. Whichever form of rate is used, when a positive NPV is obtained then the project will be worthwhile. However, other criteria may need to be considered.

Internal Rate of Return (IRR)

NPV is most frequently used in investment appraisal for acquisition purposes, but it can also be used for analysis on a trial-and-error basis.

More often, though, analysts require to know the actual return on capital to be obtained from an investment. This is the rate generated internally from the income and expenditure incurred, and therefore it is known as the Internal Rate of Return (IRR). It is the discount rate at which the NPV of income equals the NPV of expenditure, or in other words the rate which produces a nil NPV.

If for assets *A* and *B* in examples 3.4 and 3.5 the target rate had been 10%, as each produced a positive NPV it means both were generating returns above the target rate. A negative NPV would have indicated that the target rate would not have been achieved.

The IRR may be obtained by use of a computer or programmable calculator, or in some situations the 11th edition of *Parry's Tables*. In the event of neither being available then it can be calculated, by use of formula or graphically; both methods require the selection of two discount rates, one giving a positive NPV, the other a negative NPV, and then interpolating between the two.

Example 3.6

Asset *A* (example 3.4):

Year		PV £1 @ 10%	DCF	PV £1 @ 14%	DCF
0	−20,000	1	−£20,000	1	−£20,000
1	3,000	0.909	2,727	0.877	2,631
2	5,000	0.826	4,130	0.769	3,845
3	6,000	0.751	4,506	0.675	4,050
4	3,000				
	−1,000	0.683	1,366	0.592	1,184
5	6,500	0.621	4,037	0.519	3,373
6	5,750	0.564	3,243	0.456	2,622
7	3,000				
	1,500	0.513	2,308	0.400	1,800
		NPV @ 10%	£2,317	NPV @ 14%	−£495

As NPV at 10% is positive and at 14% is negative, and the IRR is the rate at which NPV is zero, then IRR will be at a rate between 10% and 14%. It can be calculated by linear interpolation which can be undertaken by using the formula:

$$R_1 + \left[(R_2 - R_1) \times \frac{NPV\ R_1}{NPV\ R_2 + NPV\ R_1} \right]$$

where: R_1 = lower rate; $NPV\ R_1$ = NPV lower rate;
R_2 = higher rate; $NPV\ R_2$ = NPV higher rate.
  In both cases, the + or − signs are ignored.

Inserting the data from above:

$$10 + \left[(14 - 10) \times \frac{2317}{495 + 2317} \right] = 13.3\%$$

Using 13.3% as IRR:

Year		PV £1 @ 13.3%	DCF
0	−20,000	1	−£20,000
1	3,000	0.883	2,649
2	5,000	0.779	3,895
3	6,000	0.688	4,128
4	3,000		
	−1,000	0.607	1,214
5	6,500	0.536	3,484
6	5,750	0.473	2,719
7	3,000		
	1,500	0.417	1,876
		NPV @13.3%	−£33

This can be demonstrated graphically on the basis of similar triangles (see figure 3.2).

$$\frac{x}{2317} = \frac{4}{495 + 2317}$$

$$x = \frac{4}{495 + 2317} \times 2317$$

$$x = 3.3\%$$

$$10\% + 3.3\% = 13.3\%$$

That the NPV is not quite zero is due to rounding of decimal places, however for analytical purpose an IRR of, say, 13.25% might be of sufficient accuracy.

However, the method is not completely accurate. Plotting Present Values as a graph produces a parabolic curve not a straight line, but again this order of accuracy is usually sufficient. By choosing rates closer together, a more accurate result will be obtained as can be seen from the following illustration.

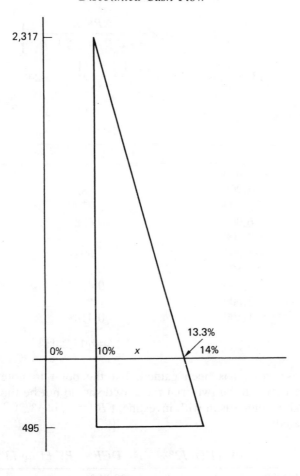

Figure 3.2

Year		PV £1 @ 13%	DCF	PV £1 @ 14%	DCF
0	−20,000	1	−£20,000	1	−£20,000
1	3,000	0.885	2,655	0.877	2,631
2	5,000	0.783	3,915	0.769	3,845
3	6,000	0.693	4,158	0.675	4,050
4	3,000				
	−1,000	0.613	1,226	0.592	1,184
5	6,500	0.543	3,529	0.519	3,372
6	5,750	0.480	2,760	0.456	2,622
7	3,000				
	1,500	0.425	1,912	0.400	1,800
		NPV @ 13%	£155	NPV @ 14%	−£495

$$R_1 + \left[(R_2 - R_1) \times \frac{NPV\ R_1}{NPV\ R_2 + NPV\ R_1} \right]$$

$$13 + \left[(14 - 13) \times \frac{155}{495 + 155} \right] = 13.24\%$$

Using 13.24% as IRR:

Year		PV £1 @ 13.24%	DCF
0	−20,000	1	−£20,000
1	3,000	0.8831	2,649.3
2	5,000	0.7798	3,899
3	6,000	0.6887	4,132.2
4	3,000		
	−1,000	0.6081	1,216.2
5	6,500	0.5370	3,490.5
6	5,750	0.4742	2,726.65
7	3,000		
	1,500	0.4188	1,884.6
		NPV @13.24%	−£1.55

In this case, little has been gained; but the point to note is that the difference between the two trial rates used should not be too great.

To make a comparison with investment *B* (example 3.5), its IRR must be calculated:

Year		PV £1 @ 12%	DCF	PV £1 @ 13%	DCF
0	−20,000	1	−£20,000	1	−£20,000
1	2,500	0.893	2,233	0.885	2,213
2	3,000	0.797	2,391	0.783	2,349
3	4,750	0.712	3,382	0.693	3,292
4	5,750	0.636	3,657	0.613	3,525
5	6,500	0.567	3,686	0.543	3,530
6	7,000	0.507	3,549	0.480	3,360
7	4.500	0.452	2,034	0.425	1,913
8	3,000	0.404	1,212	0.376	1,128
		NPV @ 12%	£394	NPV @ 13%	−£442

$$R_1 + \left[(R_2 - R_1) \times \frac{NPV\ R_1}{NPV\ R_2 + NPV\ R_1} \right]$$

$$12 + \left[(13 - 12) \times \frac{394}{442 + 394} \right] = 12.47\%$$

Using 12.47% as IRR:

Year		PV £1 @ 12.47%	DCF
0	−20,000	1	−£20,000
1	2,500	0.889	2,223
2	3,000	0.791	2,373
3	4,750	0.703	3,339
4	5,750	0.625	3,594
5	6,500	0.556	3,614
6	7,000	0.494	3,458
7	4,500	0.439	1,976
8	3,000	0.391	1,172
		NPV @12.47%	−£2

Summary

	Asset A	Asset B
Cash flow	£4,529	£4,703
DCF	£2,318	£2,189
IRR	13.25%	12.47%

It can be seen that though the cash flow from *B* is higher, *A* has a higher DCF and generates a 0.75% higher return on capital invested. Of course there might be other criteria that the investor may wish to consider.

ANALYSIS OF GILTS

IRR can be used to analyse dated Government Securities.

Consider 10% 2004 Treasury Stock in May 1990. This stock was quoted as:

Purchase price £89.625
Interest only yield 11.16%
Gross redemption yield 11.54%

Such stock is purchased in £100 bonds on which £10 will be received annually and subsequently bought back by the Treasury at face value in 2004.

Analysis:

$$\text{Initial yield} = \frac{\text{income}}{\text{purchase price}} \times 100$$

$$= \frac{£10}{89.625} \times 100$$

$$= 11.16\%$$

This could also be referred to as the 'interest only' yield because no consideration has been given to the receipt of £100 in 14 years' time. When this is brought into the cash flow and discounted, the true yield can be calculated.

Cash flow	Multiplier @ 11%	PV	Multiplier @ 12%	PV
−£89.625	1	−£89.625	1	−£89.625
£10 p.a.	YP 14 yrs 6.982	69.82	YP 14 yrs 6.628	66.28
£100	PV £1 14 yrs 0.0232	23.20	PV £1 14 yrs 0.0205	20.5
	NPV @ 11%	£3.395	NPV @ 12%	−£2.845

$$R_1 + \left[(R_2 - R_1) \times \frac{NPV\ R_1}{NPV\ R_2 + NPV\ R_1} \right]$$

$$11 + \left[(12 - 11) \times \frac{3.395}{2.845 + 3.395} \right] = 11.54\%$$

IRR = 11.54%

This could also be referred to as the Redemption Yield, because the return of capital has been taken into account. More correctly, it should be regarded as the Gross Redemption Yield because the expenses incurred in acquisition and disposal have not been included.

INCREMENTAL ANALYSIS

There will be occasions where analysis will present a position where a project having a relatively high NPV will be found to have a relatively lower IRR.

Example 3.7

Two projects have been estimated to produce the following cash flows:

	Project X	Project Y
Year 0	−£36,000	−£54,000
1	13,000	15,500
2	14,000	18,750
3	18,000	20,000
4	18,000	23,000
5		23,000

The net present value calculation using a 20% target rate is:

Year	Flow	Project X PV £1 @ 20%	PV Flow	Flow	Project Y PV £1 @ 20%	PV Flow
0	−£36,000	1	−£36,000	−£54,000	1	−£54,000
1	13,000	0.833	10,829	15,500	0.833	12,912
2	14,000	0.694	9,716	18,750	0.694	13,013
3	18,000	0.579	10,422	20,000	0.579	11,580
4	18,000	0.482	8,676	23,000	0.482	11,086
5				23,000	0.402	9,246
	NPV		£3,643			£3,837

As Project Y has the higher NPV, it would be the preferred investment. However, on calculating the IRR of each project it will be found that Project X has an IRR of 24.93% whereas Project Y is only 22.97%:

Year	Flow	Project X PV £1 @ 24.93%	PV Flow	Flow	Project Y PV £1 @ 22.97	PV Flow
0	−£36,000	1	−£36,000	−£54,000	1	−£54,000
1	13,000	0.800	10,400	15,500	0.813	12,602
2	14,000	0.641	8,974	18,750	0.661	12,394
3	18,000	0.513	9,234	20,000	0.538	10,760
4	18,000	0.411	7,398	23,000	0.437	10,051
5				23,000	0.356	8,188
	NPV		£6			−£5

Thus from an IRR point of view, Project X should have preference.

Assistance in determining the preferred investment will be given by calculating the incremental cash flows between each project. This is done by calculating the difference between each period cash flow for both projects, first by deducting Y from X then X from Y. The IRR is then calculated for each set of incremental cash flows, as follows:

Year	$X - Y$		Incremental cash flow	$Y - X$		Incremental cash flow
0	−£36,000–	(−54,000)	£18,000	−£54,000–	(−36,000)	−£18,000
1	13,000–	15,500	−2,500	15,500–	13,000	2,500
2	14,000–	18,750	−4,750	18,750–	14,000	4,750
3	18,000–	20,000	−2,000	20,000–	18,000	2,000
4	18,000–	23,000	−5,000	23,000–	18,000	5,000
5	0–	23,000	−23,000	23,000–	0	23,000
		IRR	20.34%			20.34%

The IRR for both sets of incremental flows will, of course, be the same, as follows:

Year	PV £1 @ 20.34%	$X - Y$ Incremental cash flow	PV flow	$Y - X$ Incremental cash flow	PV flow
0	1	£18,000	−£18,000	−£18,000	−£18,000
1	0.831	−2,500	2,078	2,500	2,078
2	0.691	−4,750	3,282	4,750	3,282
3	0.574	−2,000	1,148	2,000	1,148
4	0.477	−5,000	2,385	5,000	2,385
5	0.396	−23,000	9,108	23,000	9,108
	NPV		−£1		£1

At this incremental IRR of 20.34% an investor will be indifferent between either investment, because both will give the same return on capital, and give a zero NPV, and therefore it is known as the 'indifferent point'. This means that, when using NPV as the basis of comparison, a discount rate higher than 20.34% means that X will be better than Y; conversely, when a discount rate below 20.34% is used then Y will be better than X. If IRR is taken as the basis of comparison then X, which has a higher IRR, will always outperform Y.

4 Interest Rates and Yields

The relationship between market rates of interest which are inclusive of inflation and real rates of interest which exclude inflation is given by the equation:

(1 + real rate of interest) × (1 + rate of general inflation)
= 1 + market interest rate

Thus

$$(1 + i)(1 + g) = (1 + e)$$

and

$$i = \frac{(1 + e)}{(1 + g)} - 1$$

where i is the real rate of interest, g is the rate of general inflation and e is the market interest rate.

The DCF approaches used earlier in the book can be used to build growth and inflation into investment calculations. It is important, however, to consider a number of points of principle of how interest rates are made up, and how growth and inflation are built into these rates, before we can proceed further.

As outlined above, there is a need to distinguish real growth in income or rents from inflationary increases. If growth in rental income is 6% and inflation is running at 7%, then the real growth rate is negative. In fact, using the calculation above:

$$i = \frac{(1 + e)}{(1 + g)} - 1$$

Here, let us use i as the real rate of growth, as a decimal, and e as the actual rate of growth, also as a decimal. Thus:

39

$$i = \frac{(1 + 0.06)}{(1 + 0.07)} - 1 = -0.0093, \text{ say } -1\%$$

Growth can only be built into certain investments. Fixed interest investments have no growth potential, they are thus considered to be inflation-prone, as inflation will erode the real value of the income over time. The benefits of income growth have established the concept of the reverse yield gap in the investment market. This reverse yield gap has established itself in the market because of the onset of inflation; it represents a preference for inflation-proof investments such as equities, rather than inflation-prone securities such as fixed interest securities and Government stock. Prior to the appearance of periods of sustained inflation, the main determinant of the interest rate which was required by investors was risk. In this situation, if we compare Government securities (gilts) with company shares (equities), then it is obvious that the investor would perceive the Government security as having less risk; thus the interest rate demanded by the investor is less. The historical yield gap was thus the difference between the lower gilt yield and the higher equity yield. With sustained inflation, the situation changed: equities were traded at lower yields than gilts and this became known as the reverse yield gap. This situation arose because the returns on Government securities were fixed and thus eroded by inflation; the value of company dividends and share prices were reflections of the asset base and profitability of the company. Profits and dividends are, to an extent, index linked through prices and costs, and as assets are revalued they should take into account increases in value due to inflation.

Using the equation above, it should be possible to analyse this reverse yield gap. If the yield on undated gilts (we use undated gilts here, otherwise we have to deal with the possible redemption or cashing in of the stock) is 10% and the general rate of inflation is 5%, what initial return would we expect on equities? In this simplified example, we are suggesting that the investor will accept a lower return initially in the knowledge that the investment will grow and thus offset inflation. Again, let us ignore the problem of risk, by assuming that both are viewed as being of equal risk.

Let the inflation-prone rate be e (the market rate) and the initial inflation-proof rate be i (the real rate), here g is 5%. Thus:

$$i = \frac{(1 + 0.1)}{(1 + 0.05)} - 1 = 0.0476, \text{ say } 4.8\%$$

The reverse yield gap here is 5.2% and roughly equates with the inflation rate.

The traditional approach to property examines rack rental at existing levels and purports to build into the all risks yield the inflation or growth element; the two may not be the same but the approach to building them into the interest rate is. How do we assess these initial all risks yields? Take the example of the return on prime shops: if, as in the previous example, the risk-free rate of return on inflation-prone gilts is 10%, why are shops yielding 4%? Firstly, note the reverse yield gap here of 6%; this suggests that the investor is hoping for the balance to be made up in growth, which will also take inflation into account. Strictly speaking, if the two investments are comparable in terms of risk then in a perfect market situation, the main difference between the two will be the inflation allowance, and thus initially the gap is an inflation allowance. However, over time the yield may underperform or overperform relative to inflation, and this consideration may be built into the initial yield as a risk element.

This example will thus provide us with the implied growth or inflation allowance. Thus:

$$0.04 = \frac{(1 + 0.1)}{(1 + g)} - 1$$

Re-arranging:

$$(1 + g) = \frac{1.1}{1.04} = 1.0577, \text{ so } g = \text{say } 5.8\%$$

Finally, just to complete the picture, there are now index-linked Government securities. These obviously deal with the problem of both inflation and risk, and thus the initial yield being obtained reflects the time preference of money; this reflects the fact that the investor is giving up immediate consumption by spending the money and in delaying consumption is asking for an income to recompense. Thus if the initial rate on index-linked gilts is 4%, this would reflect the time-preference element. This rate is obviously dependent on the current economic conditions and future changes in economic conditions; for instance, the proportion of disposable income saved and the potential for investment may reflect this.

In the foregoing paragraphs, we have made attempts to analyse the components of the interest rate or yield. To summarise, we have identified three components: an element which provides compensation for the time preference of money, a second element related to inflation which exists to maintain the real value of the return, and finally an element of risk.

TIME-PREFERENCE ELEMENT

This exists as a compensation to the investor who now cannot spend the investment monies immediately but will need to wait until he liquefies the investment. The compensation stems from the premise that people prefer to have money now and not later – the money after all may be put to use either in consumption or alternative investment, and thus immediate satisfaction or alternative investment opportunities are obtained. The interest rate needs an element to entice people to part with their monies and delay consumption or to compete with alternative investment. From the analysis above, the rate on index-linked Treasury stock is a measure of this. Ignoring redemption, the interest rate has the elements of risk (none) and inflation covered; it thus represents an indication of the time-preference element. This rate varies with market conditions, but for ease of calculation we have assumed a 3% allowance in the calculations below.

INFLATION

It is important that this figure used in interest rates is a reflection of investors' anticipation of the inflation rate, which may differ from the expectations of the rate used by the Government, first because various financial advisors may be using different economic models to advise the Government, and secondly because the investors' index of inflation may differ from the one used by the Government. This can be exemplified by recent announcements of the Government's intention to change the basis on which the index of inflation is calculated by ignoring mortgage interest. It may be that this confuses monetary policy in that interest rate changes then feed directly into the index by changes in mortgage repayments, but mortgage interest also represents a major part of the expenditure of owner occupiers and thus should be represented in the basket of goods whose prices are measured for the inflation index. Thus the basket could be changed depending on the nature of the investor. Our calculation of a possible inflation allowance can be assessed for the investors' view of the difference between index linked gilts and ordinary undated Treasury stock. The calculation is a repeat of the exercise in the reverse yield gap above:

$$i = \frac{(1 + e)}{(1 + g)} - 1$$

Here, let us use i as the inflation-proof yield rate (index-linked, say 3%) and e as the inflation-prone rate of undated ordinary Government stock (say 10%). Thus:

$$0.03 = \frac{(1 + 0.1)}{(1 + g)} - 1$$

$$(1 + g) = \frac{1.1}{1.04} = 1.0577, \text{ so } g = \text{say } 5.8\%$$

The returns on index-linked Government stock are shown in financial newspapers, as is the rate for undated stock; the latter is listed as consols, being an abbreviation of consolidated loan stock (the Government national debt).

RISK PREMIUM

Much work has been done in the property and other investment sectors on this question of a risk premium. This is the addition to the risk-free interest rate to take into account the risk of the investment. This risk may relate to the inability to predict the level of return and perhaps the likelihood of payment.

The relationship between risk and return is direct – for instance, the monetary rewards of a Polytechnic lecturer may be low to reflect the security of his or her position (this is probably an historic analysis), while a market-maker in the City of London may obtain colossal earnings if successful in trading but runs the risk of being made redundant if earnings fall. A person investing in a Building Society will not expect very high rates of interest as the investor believes the investment to be secure, on the other hand, the person running drugs into Singapore may request large returns to cover the risk of a potential early end to his or her career.

This relationship between risk and reward is called the Capital Market Line, being the price on the market for raising capital given different risk rates. This line can be represented diagrammatically as shown below, but note that the relationship between the two may not be a simple linear one (that is, not a straight line function).

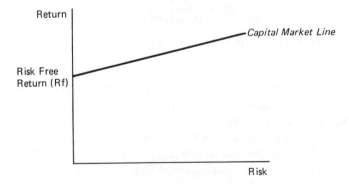

This premium arises because as investments go into the future, the outcome becomes less and less known as the time-period extends. Property projects and investments have long time-spans and thus this is an important consideration. The premium depends on the judgement of the risk involved, and this is covered in more detail in chapter 8. A comparison of rates might be obtained by taking the same investor and using him or her to borrow monies for an investment. If the first investment is risk-free, say for purchase of gilts, and the investor is risk-free from the banks' point of view, then they may offer monies at, say, Base Rate plus 2%, while another project which is less attractive may attract funds at Base Rate plus 4%; thus the risk premium to the latter project is 2%.

The problem of analysing interest rates is that there are three variables and three unknowns. However, if we make an allowance for time preference and inflation using best estimates from data available, the major variable of the risk premium can be calculated.

Example 4.1

The initial yield on prime shop property is 4%, assuming inflation to be 7% and the time-preference element to be 3%. What is the risk premium and what is the market risk-prone yield?

The risk premium is 4% less 3%, comparing the risky investment with a non-risky one which are both inflation-proof. To find the market risk-prone yield, we need to find the risk-free market rate and we build this from the formula:

$$i = \frac{(1 + e)}{(1 + g)} - 1$$

Here let us use i as the inflation-proof yield rate (3%) and e as the inflation-prone market rate; g is 7%. Thus:

$$0.03 = \frac{(1 + e)}{(1 + 0.07)} - 1$$

$$(1 + e) = 1.03 \times 1.07 = 1.11, \text{ so } e = \text{ say } 11\%$$

This inflation-prone yield rate reflects the yield on undated Government securities. If we add the 1% risk premium, this is 12%. So this yield reflects time preference, inflation and risk. If the growth of the investment is such that it outperforms the time-preference element and inflation and risk elements (assuming all remain static throughout), then there is a superprofit over and above the normal return calculated for these elements. Thus the importance of growth as distinguished from inflation is that there is an element of superprofit or potential loss in the actual growth. Even if a growth rate is included in the original appraisal (that is, an implied growth rate rather than an inflation rate), then the actual growth can still be compared with the predicted one. There is an important proviso, that if the implied growth takes care of the time-preference, inflation and risk elements, it can then have an additional superprofit built in.

The term 'superprofit' is used here to denote a return over and above the normal return. In economics, normal profit is included as a cost and superprofit in a free market will only be obtained in the short run as new entrants to the market exploit opportunities. In a perfect property market, expectations of a superprofit would encourage bidders for the investment and thus, as prices increase, the initial yield would decrease until the potential for the superprofit would decrease.

If investors need to know what return they require, then this can be worked out using the analysis above. It is important to assess the rate in terms of the requirement rather than the best available; if the rate does not come up to expectation, then it may be better to keep monies liquid rather than invest.

FLOWCHART THROUGH THE ANALYSIS OF AN INTEREST RATE

WHAT RETURN DO I WANT?
that is, WHAT IS MY EQUATED YIELD?
(this is composed of an initial yield plus growth)
(IRR with growth in income)

↓

I WANT MY YIELD TO COVER:

(i) Compensation for not being able to use the money (return for time preference)   say 3%
    plus   +
(ii) Inflation, otherwise the purchasing power of the income received will be eroded   say 7%
    plus   +
(iii) Reward for taking a risk, which will depend on the extent of the risk involved   say 3%
    equals   ———

TARGET YIELD/EQUATED YIELD   13%

↓

WHAT RETURN WILL I GET FROM PROPERTY?

(i) I want 13%

(ii) If the initial yield on prime shops is 4%, then I need a growth rate of approximately 9% (you need to use the equation outlined earlier in the chapter for the precise amount). Note that this growth rate is the money growth rate, and the real growth rate is reduced from 9% by the inflation rate of 7% to approximately 2%

or

(iii) The anticipated growth rate in rents is 6% so if I want 13% equated yield, I will buy only if the initial yield is 7% or above.

The analysis of interest rates can be used in a DCF analysis with growth, otherwise known as the calculation of the equated yield.

The steps in this calculation are as follows:

1. You build-in the anticipated growth rate into the cash flows. Use the IRR technique to find the equated yield (this is fully explained in chapter 5).
2. You then compare the equated yield produced with other investments: for example

	Inflation	Time preference	Risk	Equated yield
Gilts	7%	3%	0%	= 10%
Prime property	7%	3%	1%	= 11%

3. If the yield produced in 1 is greater than the target equated yield in 2, then you would invest in prime property; if not, then you would invest in Gilts.

5 Equated Yields

The equated yield is the yield on a property investment which takes into account growth in future income. (This is not applicable to reversionary situations, where the increase in income on reversion is to the market value as estimated at the present time.)

Variables in the analysis of the equated yield are:

(i) Initial yield (all risks yield) that is, for a freehold $= \dfrac{\text{rack rent}}{\text{purchase price}}$ (I)

(ii) Annual growth rate of rent (G)

(iii) Rent review period (n)

(iv) Equated yield (E)

In any investment situation, I and n are known, G can be estimated to find E or E can be a target yield and thus the relevant G found.

Equated yield analysis merely links these variables together in a formula. The formula is explained later in the chapter but first the underlying approach must be explained using discounted cash flow techniques developed in chapter 3.

EQUATED YIELD ANALYSIS

The internal rate of return technique used in discounted cash flow calculations can be applied to investments where rents vary. It can be applied where there is a term and reversion situation to find an overall yield, and this is called the 'equivalent yield' which is considered in chapter 7. It can also be applied to rack rented freeholds to take into account growth on rent review, called the 'equated yield'. Thus the difference between the two is that equated yields deal with rents into which a growth factor has been included.

The technique of equated yield analysis is as follows:

1. Assume a growth rate in the rental per annum. Apply this to the original income using the Amount of £1. You can use the table from *Parry's* to find this or the equation $A = (1 + i)^n$, where A is the amount that £1 accumulates at the compound interest rate $i\%$ p.a. over n years. In this case you insert the growth rate as i and the new rent including growth will be the original rent multiplied by A.

   For example, the original rent is £10,000 p.a. Assuming a growth rate of 10% p.a., the new rent after five years inclusive of growth is £10,000 × A or £10,000 × $(1 + 0.10)^5$ = £16,105

   Or from *Parry's Tables*:

   new rent is £10,000 × Amount of £1 in 5 years @ 10% (1.6105) = £16,105.

2. You put the income with growth into the DCF analysis, that is:

Year	Income	*Trial rate 16%*		NPV
		YP for 5 years @ 16%	PV £1 @ 16%	
1–5	£10,000			
6–10	£16,105			

and so on. Once the IRR has been found, this is the equated yield.

Example 5.1

A freehold investment has been purchased for £100,000; it has a rack rental value of £5,000 p.a. It is let on a lease for 25 years with 5 year reviews. Assuming rental growth of 10% p.a., determine the equated yield.

   The layout below is a possible presentation of the calculation if you were to use a computer spreadsheet. See chapter 14 for an introduction to the use of computer spreadsheets in the analysis.

Calculation of Equated Yield:

Capital Value	£100,000	
Initial Rent	£5,000 p.a.	
Initial Yield/YP	5%	20 YP
Trial Equated Yields	14%	15%
Rent Review Frequency	5 yearly	
Growth Rate p.a.	10% compound	
YP for review period at Trial Rate	3.433081	3.352155

(These YPs are based on YP for 5 years (review period) at the trial rates of 14% and 15%, as above.)

Period (years)	Amt £1 @ 10%	Cash flow	PV £1 14%	Deferred YP	PV of slice
0		−100,000			−100,000
1–5	n/a	5,000	n/a	3.433081	17,165
6–10	1.610510	8,053	0.5193687	1.783035	14,358
11–15	2.593742	12,969	0.2697438	0.9260523	12,010
16–20	4.177248	20,886	0.1400965	0.4809626	10,046
21–25	6.727500	33,637	0.0727617	0.2497969	8,403
26–30	10.83471	54,174	0.0377902	0.1297367	7,028
31–perp	17.44940	87,247	0.0196270	0.3925405	34,248

Net present value   3,257

Period (years)	Amt £1 @ 10%	Cash flow	PV £1 15%	Deferred YP	PV of slice
0		−100,000			−100,000
1–5	n/a	5,000	n/a	3.352155	16,761
6–10	1.610510	8,053	0.4971767	1.666614	13,420
11–15	2.593742	12,969	0.2471847	0.8286015	10,746
16–20	4.177248	20,886	0.1228945	0.4119614	8,604
21–25	6.727500	33,637	0.0611003	0.2048176	6,890
26–30	10.83471	54,174	0.0303776	0.1018306	5,517
31–perp	17.44940	87,247	0.0151031	0.3020611	26,354

Net present value   − 11,709

$$\text{IRR} = 14 + \left(1 \times \frac{3{,}257}{14{,}966} \right) = 14.22$$

Notes to calculation

1. Because the rent review period is for 5 years, the calculation deals with the cash flows in slices of 5 years as the income cannot change within the 5 year period.
2. The cash flows for each period have been inflated by the amount of £1 at the growth rate of 10% to the beginning of each period, showing the rent with growth at each review.

3. The deferral rate is calculated for each cash flow period for each trial rate (PV £1 for deferred period at 14 and 15%).
4. The period cash flow is valued by capitalising at the trial rates for the 5 year period (YP 5 years at 14 and 15%). This is multiplied by the PV £1 column to give the deferred YP.
5. The deferred YP at the trial rates is multiplied by the inflated cash flow to give the value of the deferred slice. The values of the deferred slices are added together to give the net present value.
6. To calculate the equated yield which is the IRR of the calculation, we need to arrive at a positive and negative NPV and interpolate between them to obtain the point where NPV = 0; this is then the yield which is the IRR.
7. The calculation could go on to infinity, but cash flows after 30 years because of the deferred factor make little difference. The calculation is cut short at 30 years; after this, no growth is added to the income and thus we can resort to the initial yield for both trial rates. In this case, the initial yield is 5% and the final deferred YP is YP in perpetuity @ 5% deferred 30 years. In view of the problems of predicting growth after a period, it may be more desirable to limit the analysis to 20 years.

The calculation seems complex. The first thing to note is that it is a basic IRR calculation with two trial rates; the second point is that the cash flows have to be dealt with in slices – the cash flows could be dealt with individually but this seems pointless if the flows remain unchanged for the review period. As we have seen, the Year's Purchase is the present value of £1 p.a. and this can be used to do the calculation for the period of unchanged rent for us. To clarify further, take out a slice and see what happens. Taking the period for years 11–15, the original rent will have grown for 10 years before the review in year 10 (assuming the 5 year reviews in the example). Thus:

Original rent	£5,000 p.a.
Amt of £1 @ 10%	2,593742
Expected rent	£12,969 p.a.

This rent will run for a 5 year period to the next review, so we can capitalise it using a Year's Purchase. We use the trial rate for discounting and as the Year's Purchase will discount a stream of income to present values, we use this to discount the stream between the review dates. Let us use the trial rate of 15%:

Expected rent	£12,969
YP 5 years @ 15%	3.352155
Capital value of slice	£43,474

The value of this slice is in 10 years' time, as the YP calculation has summed the discounted cash flows in the period of years 11–15 (each has been discounted back at the rate of 15% to the beginning of year 11 and added together). Thus to get back to present value, we need to discount this capital value back 10 years:

Future value of slice	£43,474
Present value of £1 for 10 years @ 15%	0.2471847
Present value of slice	£10,746

As with the traditional methods, there are alternative ways of arriving at this solution. Tables have been constructed in the same way as *Parry's Tables* have been constructed for traditional valuations. The tables used to assess the equated yield are *Donaldson's Investment Tables* produced by Philip Marshall, and these are explained later in the chapter. A third alternative is to use the equation which underpins the tables and the analysis above.

The equated yield equation is:

$$I = E - E\left[\frac{(1 + G)^n - 1}{(1 + E)^n - 1}\right]$$

where

I is the initial yield or all risks yield which =

$$\frac{\text{rack rent}}{\text{purchase price}}$$

where property is freehold, let at the rack rent or full open market rental value. The yield is expressed as a decimal not a percentage
E is the equated yield as a decimal
G is the annual growth rate in rental income compounded as a decimal
n is the rent review period in years.

Example 5.2

Your client wants to purchase a shop investment let at a rack rent of
£100,000. Her target equated yield is 13%. You have assessed the probable
growth rate in income to be 5% p.a. compound.

Using the equation

$$I = E - E \left[\frac{(1 + G)^n - 1}{(1 + E)^n - 1} \right]$$

it is possible to value the interest assuming a 5 year rent review. Thus:

$$I = 0.13 - 0.13 \left[\frac{(1 + 0.05)^5 - 1}{(1 + 0.13)^5 - 1} \right]$$

$$= 0.13 - (0.13 \times 0.3279) = 0.873, \text{ say } 8\tfrac{3}{4}\%$$

Valuation:
Rack rent   £100,000
YP in perp. @ $8\tfrac{3}{4}\%$ 11.42
                             _____

Capital value   £1,142,000

Assuming the purchase goes ahead at the valuation, it is possible to
calculate the actual equated yield on the investment. The actual calculation
is not completed as it has been carried out above. The equated yield
calculation can be set out as follows: rents are inflated at the growth rate,
capitalised for the review period of 5 years and deferred to give a Present
Value. This deferral is carried out at two trial rates to give a positive and
negative Net Present Value as close as possible to zero, and the interpolation provides an Equated Yield based on the internal rate of return
produced. A computer spreadsheet or program would provide a more
exact answer, and sophisticated hand calculators can also provide solutions.

Example 5.3

Making any necessary assumptions and using an appropriate equated yield
together with the equation

$$I = E - E \left[\frac{(1 + G)^n - 1}{(1 + E)^n - 1} \right]$$

it is possible to value a freehold investment property as follows. We know that the property has been let recently on a 25 year lease with 5 year reviews on full repairing and insuring terms at a rental of £100,000 p.a. exclusive.

In the first case, we may need to assess the client's target equated yield which could be carried out as follows. The interest rate has three basic elements:

(1) time value element
(2) inflation element
(3) risk element.

(1) can be assessed from the yield on index linked Government stocks which have no risk and are guaranteed against inflation, say 3% p.a.
(2) can be assessed from gilt yields (consols) which carry no risk and thus reflect the inflation and time preference elements, say 10% for both elements.
(3) risk could be assessed from short-term market rates on loans from a bank, say base plus a risk rate @ 14% which when compared with (2) shows risk at 4%.

The client's equated yield could be the cost of borrowing (14%) the target yield assessed as above (3 + 7 + 4% = 14%) or the return on competing or previous schemes. See chapter 4 for further information relating to interest rate structures.

Assume equated yield = 14%
and growth = inflation @ 5%

$$I = 0.14 - 0.14 \left\{ \frac{(1 + 0.05)^5 - 1}{(1 + 0.14)^5 - 1} \right\}$$

$$= 0.14 - 0.14 \times 0.2986 = 0.0982, \text{ say } 9.8\%$$

Valuation:
rack rent	£100,000
YP in perp. @ 9.8%	10.2
Capital value	£1,020,000

The third approach to equated yield analysis as mentioned previously, is to look at *Donaldson's Investment Tables*. The tables allow you to look up the equated yield for the variables of rent review period (3, 5, 7, 14, 25, yearly), the growth rate (5%, 10% etc.) and the initial yield. The tables are arranged on the basis of growth rates, so the page is found for the relevant

growth rate, the column on the page for the appropriate review period, and
then the initial yield is found in the column; this then provides the Equated
Yield on another column. The layout appears thus:

Review   *Alternative Review Periods*
Period

5   3   7   10   14   21   25   33

Initial	*Equated*							
Yields	*Yields*			*Corresponding Initial Yields*				
3	10.6	2.80	3.21	3.53	3.97	4.73	5.16	5.97
3.25	10.81	3.03	3.48	3.82	4.29	5.10	5.56	6.40
3.5	11.03	3.26	3.74	4.11	4.61	5.47	5.94	6.82
3.75	11.25	3.50	4.01	4.40	4.93	5.83	6.33	7.23
etc. to 12%	etc.			etc.				

Example 5.4

A freehold investment has sold for £1,000,000; it was recently let at a rental
of £35,000 p.a. The lease is for 20 years with a 10 year review. Assuming a
growth rate of 8% p.a., calculate the equated yield.

The property has been recently let, so we assume the rental to be the rack
rent. The initial yield is

$$\frac{£35,000}{£1,000,000} \times 100\% = 3.5\%$$

Using Donaldson's Tables:

Method:

1. Find 8% Growth page (see table above).
2. Check 10 year rent review column.
3. Find initial yield close to 3.5; here it is 3.53.
4. Find equated yield in same row = 10.6%.

GROWTH

So far in this chapter we have considered equated yield analysis in which the initial yield (or all risks yield) (I), the growth rate of rent (G), and the rent review pattern (n, where n is the number of years between reviews) can be used to find the equated yield (E). It is also possible to use a target equated yield to find the growth rate required to obtain the target yield.

To find the growth rate, we can search *Donaldson's Tables* until we find a table that matches the initial yield (I) in the rent review pattern column required with the required equated yield (E). In the previous example, we would search the tables to match an E of 10.6 with an I (in the 10 year review column) of 3.5. The table would tell us the growth rate used on that page. It may be necessary to interpolate between figures to find a more precise growth rate.

It is also possible to work out the growth rate by formula.

$$G = \sqrt[n]{\left[1 + \frac{(E-I)}{ASF} \right]} - 1$$

where $\sqrt[n]{}$ *is the nth root of the section in square brackets.*

This can also be written:

$$G = \left[1 + \frac{(E - I)}{ASF} \right]^{\frac{1}{n}} - 1$$

Note that all figures are in decimals.

G = growth rate p.a., I = initial or all risks yield, E = equated yield, and n is the number of years between reviews.
ASF is the annual sinking fund for n years @ $E\%$; this can be found directly from *Parry's Tables* or the equation (see chapter 1) can be used.

$$ASF = \frac{i}{A - 1}, \text{ where } A \text{ is the Amount of £1} = (1 + i)^n$$

Thus

$$ASF = \frac{i}{(1 + i)^n - 1}$$

Here we said the interest rate is $E\%$, so $ASF = \dfrac{E}{(1 + E)^n - 1}$

Assuming $E = 12.5\%$, $I = 5\%$ and $n = 5$ years, then

$$G = \sqrt[5]{\left[1 + \frac{(0.125 - 0.05)}{0.156^*}\right]} - 1 = 0.82 = 8.2\%$$

$*ASF$ 5 years @ 12.5%. $ASF = \dfrac{i}{A - 1} = \dfrac{0.125}{(1 + 0.125)^5 - 1}$

VALUATIONS BY EQUATED YIELD ANALYSIS

Example 5.5

A freehold investment recently let on a lease with 5 year reviews is producing a net income of £30,000 p.a. A comparable property has been let at £30,000 p.a. recently and sold for £650,000, but is let on a 3 year review pattern. In order to value the property we need to find the initial yield of the subject property, but of the other 3 variables used in equated yield analysis we know n (number of years between reviews), but not growth rate G nor equated yield E.

In the case of the comparable property, we can work out the initial yield I and we know n, but again G and E are not known.

As G and E are both unknown, we can assume the investor's target yield in order to solve the equation. So let $E =$ say 16% (riskless rate of long-term gilts plus say 4% risk – see chapter 4 for discussions on this; the risk will depend on the nature of the investment).

Method:
1. Initial yield of comparable property is

$$\frac{£30,000 \text{ p.a.}}{£650,000} \times 100\% = 4.62\%$$

2. Assume that your investor's target equated yield is 16%.
3. Use comparable property where $E = 16\%$, $n = 3$ years and $I = 4.62\%$ to find the growth rate. *Donaldson's Tables* give say 12% (we could also use the equation above to find G).
4. Assume the growth rate is applicable to the subject property and find I for the subject property in *Donaldson's Tables* where $G = 12\%$, $n = 5$ years and $E = 16\%$. *Donaldson's Tables* will give $I = 5.1\%$.
5. Valuation:

Net income	£30,000 p.a.
YP @ 5.1%	19.6
Capital value	£588,000

Thus equated yield analysis using *Donaldson's Tables* is able to manipulate data from one rent review pattern to another. This is discussed in greater length in chapter 8 on equated rents.

YIELD DEFINITIONS

There has been much confusion between the concepts of equated and equivalent yield. In addition, the definitions of internal rate of return and the gross redemption yield on Government stock have added to the confusion. The easiest way to distinguish the yields is to consider a basic investment; the investment is purchased simply to produce a cash flow return in the future. The concept of discounting enters the analysis on the basis that income in the future is less valuable than income today. This is for the reasons set out in chapter 4, namely that there may be a risk in achieving it, there may be inflation eroding the real value of it and that it is inconvenient to defer present consumption by investing (and a rate for compensation is required). These items make up the market interest rate. In chapter 4 we discussed the nature of real and money rates. In discounting cash flows we must match the interest rate with the nature of the cash flow. Money flows must be discounted by market rates and real income flows by real rates, and you will recall that the differences between the two relate to the inclusion or not of inflation. So let us summarise the possible yield definitions:

- Internal Rate of Return
- All Risks Yield
- Equated Yield.
- Equivalent Yield
- Gross Redemption Yield.

Internal Rate of Return (IRR)

The IRR, if we refer back to chapter 3, is the rate used in discounted cash flow analysis and is the basic rate used here. It is defined as the rate at which the discounted flow will match the initial outlay, that is, the point where the Net Present Value = 0. We can take this rate as the general case. In the IRR we are discounting cash flows back at an appropriate rate. We could use real or money flows and we could also bunch the cash flows together in tranches. This approach is flexible and thus IRR is the basic analysis on which the other yields are founded.

All Risks Yield (ARY)

In a rack rented freehold, the ARY will also equal the initial yield. The ARY is the traditional yield we use in conventional valuations. If we use rack rent, we keep the rental income the same all the way through the life of the asset and we ignore the effects of inflation, growth and risk – all factors which could affect the nature of the cash flows. These aspects, though, are included in the consideration of the level of yield. The income remains at the same level and does not equate with the actual money income received in any particular year. The cash flows are real cash flows, not money flows inflated by inflation or growth, and thus the discount rate is a real rate.

Equivalent Yield

The equivalent yield is a variation on the theme of the all risks yield. The traditional approach involves capitalising the term rent at a lower rate of interest than that used for the reversionary rent. This is the overall yield attached to the term and reversion. The equivalent yield (which will be discussed in chapter 7) is the internal rate of return on the term and reversionary investment. It is a weighted average yield with no allowance being made for future rental growth. The income here is not static but restricted because of legal constraints written in the lease until it can change to market value. But the market value at review used in the analysis is the market value as at the date of valuation (as with the all risks yield) and future growth, inflation and risk are not built into the cash flows. To use another expression, the cash flows are not explicit – they do not indicate possible variations in the flows through periods of time. This is taken into account in the discount rate which, as with the all risks yield, is implicit.

Gross Redemption Yield (GRY)

The gross redemption yield is an equivalent yield applied to Government dated stocks (gilts) which provide a fixed income and then are redeemable at par or a fixed amount on expiration with no growth built in. Thus for the GRY and equivalent yield, the yields are the IRR of the cash flows without growth. For the equivalent yield, the cash flows are for a term income and a reversionary income. For a gilt, the cash flow is a fixed income over the life of the gilt and a fixed capital repayment (see chapter 7).

Equated Yield

For the calculation of the Equated Yield we use the IRR of the cash flows again, but in this case the cash flows are best estimates of what will happen and include an allowance for growth and risk, and the discount rate is a market rate discounting the money cash flows. This is the usual way that financial analysts would look at a cash flow. The difference between general investment scenarios and a property investment is that the cash flows are constrained by the lease arrangements in property and the cash flows only change on review or at the end of the lease on reletting. Cash flows in a conventional financial analysis would be free to change annually. Chapter 15 looks at aspects of financial analysis, but two important points must be clarified at this stage. These are:

1. The criteria for valuing property assets with and without growth and the choice of yield in the circumstances.
2. The relationship of property valuation to the valuation of other assets.

VALUATION WITH INCOME GROWTH

The choice of yield as outlined above is dependent on the inclusion or not of growth in the analysis, but more generally the yield or rate used will depend on the nature of the cash flow. Thus the rate matches the cash flow:

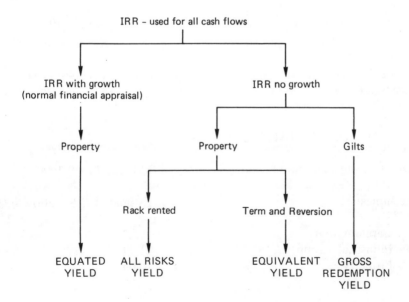

The initial yield is, of course, the all risks yield in a rack rental situation, but may be confused with a term yield in a term and reversion. For clarity, it is better to distinguish between the initial and the term yield. In practice, the use of the term 'all risks yield' for 'initial yield' would be preferable.

RELATIONSHIP BETWEEN THE VALUATION OF PROPERTY AND OTHER ASSETS

The use of cash flows generally in financial circles is based on discounting actual money flows over a period of time. The IRR is used to do this, and this is mirrored in property terms by the Equated Yield. We have seen previously how the Gross Redemption Yield is paralleled by the Equivalent Yield. There are also parallels of the all risk yield, for instance the use of the Price:Earnings (*P/E*) ratio. Basically, the value of a trading company is assessed on the market by using the latest net profits (these are subject to some adjustments, but the principles are the same) and capitalising the profits using a Price:Earnings ratio as one would use a Year's Purchase. The parallel is clearly shown as follows:

Valuation of company	*Valuation of a property*
Net profit	Net income
× *P/E* ratio	× Year's Purchase
= Capital value	= Capital value

$$P/E \text{ ratio} = \frac{\text{Market price of share}}{\text{Earnings per share}} \qquad YP = \frac{\text{Capital value}}{\text{Net income}}$$

The FT−Actuaries Share Indices in the *Financial Times* provide a compilation of the share price on any particular day, a typical entry would be:

FT–ACTUARIES SHARES INDICES

Equity Groups and Sub-Sections	Monday July 9 1990
Examples:	Estimated *P/E* Ratio (Net)
1. Capital Goods	9.22
49. Industrial Group	11.29
69. Property	16.04

There will be individual *P/E* ratios for all companies listed in the *Financial Times*. In respect of the property sector, you should note that property trading companies would be valued on an investment basis using the *P/E* ratio but that property investment companies would be valued on the basis of their net asset value (Isaac and Woodroffe, 1986).

The *P/E* ratio works in the same way as a yield: a higher *P/E* ratio or Year's Purchase represents a lower yield, and therefore what is perceived as a better investment in terms of the generation of future cash flows. To value a company in its simplest form, we take the net profit for the preceding year and capitalise it using the *P/E* ratio.

Example 5.6

Assuming a net profit of £1m and a *P/E* ratio of 16.04:

Net profit	£1,000,000 ×
P/E ratio	16.04
Market value of company	£16,040,000

If there are a million shares in the company, then assuming they are all on the same basis this would indicate that the share price to reflect the value would be £16.04p per share. This is a very simplistic approach which does not identify problems of capital structure, the relationship between share price and market capitalisation and the calculation of income to be used in the analysis. The analysis is included to provide some parallel appraisal methods, and it assists the understanding of property appraisal techniques to see these comparisons. Chapter 15 looks at profitability and company capital structure in more detail.

REFERENCE

Isaac, D. and Woodroffe, N. (1986). 'Corporate Finance and Property Development Funding', Working Paper, Polytechnic of the South Bank, London.

FURTHER READING

Enever, N., *The Valuation of Property Investments*, Estates Gazette, London, 1989.

6 Hardcore Method

This chapter is about valuing reversionary investments. A reversionary investment is where a property is let at less than full market rental but where there is a rent review or a reletting to the full market rental. This is a common occurrence where rental values have risen since the grant of the lease or rent review or where the lessee has paid a premium on entry. There are two different approaches to valuing reversionary investments: the traditional term and reversion method based on a block income approach, and the hardcore method based on a layered income approach.

CONVENTIONAL APPROACH

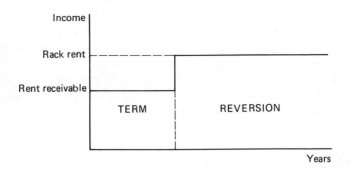

In the block income valuation, the present rent is capitalised to reversion, to give the capital value of the term. The rack rent is then capitalised in perpetuity to give the capital value of the reversion. The capital value of the investment is the values of the term and reversion added together. This has already been looked at in chapter 2.

HARDCORE (LAYER) APPROACH

In the hardcore approach, the rent currently received is capitalised in perpetuity, the incremental rent is capitalised separately and the values of

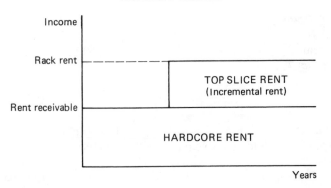

the hardcore and the increment are added together. This is based on the view that the hardcore rent is secure, so that the reviewed rent will not fall below the historic rent paid under the lease but the risk will be attached to the incremental rent to be received on reversion.

If the conventional term and reversion is using the same yield for the term and reversion, then this rate can be applied to the hardcore method to get the same result.

Example 6.1

Value the freehold interest in a commercial premises let at £6,000 p.a. net with a rent review in 4 years. The rack rental is £9,000 p.a. Assume the freehold yield at the rack rent to be 7%.

Conventional Approach:

Term
Rent received   £6,000 p.a.
YP 4 years @ 7%   3.387

                                          £20,322

Reversion to rack rent   £9,000 p.a.
YP in perp. @ 7% deferred 4 years   10.898

                                          £98,082

                     CAPITAL VALUE   £118,404

Hardcore Method:

Hardcore rent	£6,000 p.a.	
YP in perp. @ 7%	14.285	
		£85,710

Incremental rent	£3,000 p.a.	
YP in perp. @ 7% deferred 4 years	10.898	
		£32,694
	CAPITAL VALUE	£118,404

If the term yield in the conventional valuation differs from the yield used on the reversion, then there will be different results using the different methods. This would be so in situations where the term rent is less than the rack rent, and so it may be considered that the term rent is more secure and therefore should be valued at a lower yield than the reversion. The results of the conventional and hardcore methods will only coincide where the incremental rent is capitalised at an appropriate marginal rate.

Example 6.2

Value the freehold interest in a commercial premises let at £6,000 p.a. net with a rent review in 4 years. The rack rental is £9,000 p.a. Assume the freehold yield at the rack rent to be 7%. (The term yield is assumed to be 6%).

Conventional Approach:

Term		
Rent received	£5,000 p.a.	
YP 4 years @ 6%	3.485	
		£20,790

Reversion to rack rent	£9,000 p.a.	
YP in perp. @ 7% deferred 4 years	10.898	
		£98,082
	CAPITAL VALUE	£118,872

Hardcore Method:
The approach is:

Step (i)
Determine the yield on the hardcore element. The hardcore income is the same as the term income so we can use the term yield, 6%.

Step (ii)
Determine the yield on the increment to obtain the same capital value as by the conventional method:

$$\text{Yield on increment} = \frac{\text{incremental income}}{\text{capital value of increment}}$$

This statement is obvious, as yield of any investment is determined by the income divided by the capital value. In this case the incremental income is the difference between the rack rent and the hardcore rent (same as term rent). Thus

$$\text{Incremental income} = \text{rack rent} - \text{term rent}$$
$$= \pounds 9,000 - \pounds 6,000 = \pounds 3,000$$

The capital value of the increment is slightly more difficult to work out. If we look diagrammatically at the hardcore diagram, we can see that, ignoring the period before the reversion, the capital value of the increment is the difference between the capital value of the reversion less the capital value of the hardcore element.

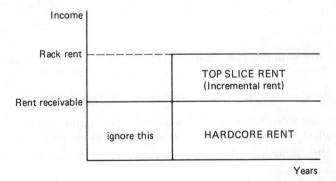

So the capital value of the rack rent in perpetuity less the capital value of the hardcore rent in perpetuity gives the value of the incremental income in perpetuity.

Rack rent	£9,000	
YP in perp. @ 7%	14.285	
	————	
		£128,565

less

Hardcore rent	£6,000	
YP in perp. @ 6%	16.66	
	————	
		£99,960
		————

CAPITAL VALUE OF INCREMENT   £28,605

Thus the yield on the increment $= \dfrac{£3,000}{£28,605} \times 100\% = 10.5\%$

Step (iii)
Complete hardcore valuation:

Hardcore rent	£6,000 p.a.	
YP in perp. @ 6%	16.66	
	————	£99,960

Incremental rent	£3,000 p.a.	
YP in perp. @ 10.5% deferred 4 years	6.388	
	————	
		£19,164
		————

CAPITAL VALUE   £119,124

This compares with the valuation of £118,872 by the traditional method.

Example 6.3

Shop premises were recently let for £10,000 per annum exclusive on a modern full repairing and insuring lease for 25 years with 5 year rent reviews. The freehold subject to the lease was subsequently sold for £125,000.

You have been asked by a client to value the freehold interest in a comparable shop nearby let on a full repairing and insuring lease for 25 years with 5 year reviews, 2 years ago. The current rent is £7,000 p.a. with an increase to full market rental at the next rent review.

Hardcore Approach:

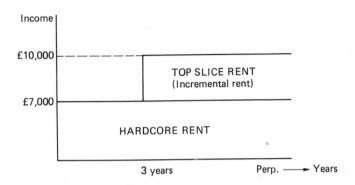

The hardcore valuation values each layer. From the comparable property, the yield at rack rent is 8% so the term yield in a traditional valuation would be, say, 7% and this equals the hardcore yield. The incremental rent is riskier so this yield is, say, 12% (you would really need comparable properties to assess this).

Valuation:
Hardcore rent	£7,000	
YP in perp. @ 7%	14.85	
		£100,030
Incremental rent	£3,000	
YP in perp. @12% deferred 3 yrs	5.93	
		£17,790
Capital value		£117,820 say £118,000

At review, market rent could fall; this approach values the risk in the top slice while appreciating that a tenant's existing rent is secure. (However, this approach does not allow for inflation, and the income does not reflect potential growth.)

By adjustment of the incremental yield it is possible to achieve the same capital value as by the traditional term and reversion method:

$$\text{Incremental yield} = \frac{\text{incremental income}}{\text{capital value of incremental income}}$$

The incremental income = £10,000 p.a. − £7,000 p.a. = £3000 p.a.

The capital value of incremental income = capital value of the rack rent in perp. − capital value of the hardcore rent in perp.

To find the capital value of the incremental income:

Rack rent	£10,000	
YP in perp. @ 8%	12.5	
	———	
Capital value of rack rent		£125,000
less Hardcore rent	£7,000	
YP in perp. @ 7%	14.85	
	———	
Capital value of hardcore rent		£99,995
Capital value of incremental income		£25,005

$$\text{Yield on incremental rent} = \frac{£3,000}{£25,005} \times 100\% = 12\%$$

Using this yield in the hardcore valuation would give the same result as the traditional term and reversion at 7% term yield and 8% reversion yield.

Andrew Trott (1986) in the RICS/South Bank Polytechnic research into property valuation methods suggests the following advantages and disadvantages of the hardcore method:

Advantages
1. The increase in capital value of an investment due to the extra rent receivable upon rent review or reversion can be calculated.
2. It isolates the less secure top-slice income from the safer hardcore rent. In the volatile market of the early 1970s, the method seemed an appropriate tool to value the uncertain top-slice income.
3. It is especially suitable in the valuation of turnover rents.
4. It can be used to deal with tax-free capital appreciation.
5. It is sometimes used to minimise the problems of capital recoupment associated with the conventional valuation of variable profit rents. There is only an advantage, however, if either the hardcore or marginal rent exceeds the other by a considerable amount.

Disadvantages
1. It invokes the artificial division of income. The security of the reversion-

ary income is not divisible; if the tenant defaults in the payment of the marginal income, then he defaults in the payment of the hardcore income.
2. It does not directly use the market based ARY (all risks yield or initial yield) since the hardcore rent is valued at a lower yield than the ARY while the marginal income is valued at a higher rate.
3. Material discrepancies between the hardcore and term and reversion methods can occur where the term income is substantially below the current full market rental value.

These criticisms tend to overstate the problems of the method. In a poor investment market, which is the outlook for the early 1990s as was the fact for the 1970s, the ability to analyse the risk in the top-slice income is very important especially where, because of a downturn in the market, the expected increment may not be achieved. A contractual agreement to a rent above the market rent is risky for the tenant and puts the tenant in a poor position with competitors, thus a revision of the rent or negotiation may stabilise the position and if the parties are flexible we are actually looking at a division of the income here. The hardcore method is linked to the all risks yield and this is a fundamental concept in how the approach has developed; the traditional method uses a reversionary rack rented yield and a term yield related to this (say 1% less for security), and although there may be a debate about the yield to be used on the term, the hardcore yield actually lifts this directly from the traditional method. Finally, there are bound to be discrepancies if you use a different method; the argument is whether or not it is a better method and more a reflection of transactions in the market. If comparable properties are analysed over a period using the hardcore method, then these can be used to determine the incremental yield directly.

The method has also been criticised as tending to overvalue the hardcore income in the sense that the secure term yield is used throughout the life of the asset. This may lead to an undervaluation of the increment but only if the overall valuation is matched to a traditional term and reversion; otherwise it may or may not, depending on the incremental yield used. W. A. Leach (1978), in his analysis of the approach, reaches the conclusion that the hardcore method is invalid since it manufactures fictitious circumstances in which to value (see the disadvantages discussed above). In our view, by reflecting the effect of risk on the cash flows it is looking at a variable that is useful and has useful parallels in other areas. The flow of income from any project could come in various forms. The key criteria for the flows are the amount of the flow related to the risk; the hardcore method is a reflection in an investment property of layering returns from a development situation (in partnership schemes, for instance, see Darlow, 1988). It also reflects the way profits are distributed in companies (debt and equity returns, see chapter 16) or in a more complex form the securitisation of property assets such as Billingsgate (based on the corporate structure discussed in chapter 16). It thus assists in focusing attention away from the mechanics of the valuation to the economic context which can affect the investment drastically.

The method must be important in a declining market, especially in situations where contractual arrangements force the rent payable above the rack rent or where a property in a specific location experiences adverse forces (the completion of a nearby competing shopping centre, for instance) which may lead to a decrease in the rent obtainable. Graphically, these variations may appear as follows.

Contractual arrangements to pay above the market value:

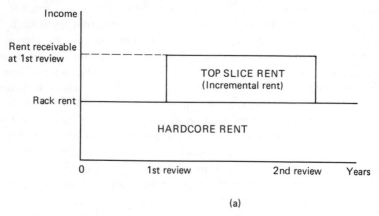

(a)

This assumes property is let at present rack rent.

Possibility of rent decrease on review:

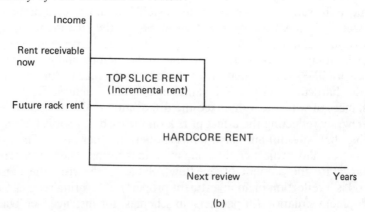

(b)

This assumes property is let at present rack rent.

REFERENCES

Darlow, C. (ed.) (1988). *Valuation and Development Appraisal*, Estates Gazette, London, Chapter 2.

Leach, W. A. (1978). *Hardcore Method of Valuation*, Estates Gazette, London, May 6, p. 475.

Trott, A. (ed.) (1986). 'Property Valuation Methods', Research Report, Royal Institution of Chartered Surveyors/Polytechnic of the South Bank, July.

7 Equivalent Yields

Reversionary investments can be valued by the traditional or the hardcore methods. However, investors may require to know the overall yield. For instance, if the term is valued at 6% and the reversion is valued at 8%, what is the overall yield of the investment? The equivalent yield is thus the weighted average yield. It is the internal rate of return on the cash flows used for the term and reversion. You should note that these cash flows are at current rental values, not inflated for growth. Thus the calculation of the equivalent yield differs from the equated yield in this respect. Chapter 5 has already looked at the difference between yields. The equivalent yield, in providing an overall yield, means that reversionary property has a single yield which can be compared with the returns on other investments, either property or non-property.

If the yields used on the term and reversion are the same, then the equivalent yield is the same. The following example assumes that the term rent is more secure and thus attracts a lower yield.

Example 7.1

A shop is let at £5,000 p.a. net. The rack rent is £20,000 p.a. There are 3 years to go on the lease. Calculate the equivalent yield on the freehold reversionary interest.

Traditional Approach:

Term		
Rent reserved	£5,000	
YP 3 yrs @ 5%	2.723	
		£13,615
Reversion		
Rack rental	£20,000	
YP in perp. deferred 3 yrs @ 7%	11.661	
		£233,220
Capital value		£246,835

The calculation of the equivalent yield is possible by three methods:

(1) by formula
(2) by DCF
(3) by reference to tables (either *Parry's* or *Donaldson's*). For clarity and because this approach is relatively straightforward, we will not discuss the latter method here.

Solution by formula:

$$\text{Equivalent Yield} = \frac{(\text{Present income} + \text{annual equivalent of gain}) \times 100}{\text{Price}}$$

Here the present income is £5,000 and the price is the capital value assessed above, £246,835.

$$\text{Annual equivalent of the gain} = \frac{\text{gain on reversion} \times \text{PV £1 for term}}{\text{YP for term}}$$

The gain on reversion is the difference between the value on reversion and the present value (price).

Thus the value on reversion is calculated:

Rack rental	£20,000
YP in perp. @ 7%	14.285
	£285,700

The gain on reversion is £285.700 − £246,835 = £38,865.
  The annual equivalent of the gain is

$$\frac{£38,865 \times \text{PV £1 @ 6.5\% in 3 years}}{\text{YP 3 years @ 6.5\%}}$$

The rate used in the calculation is a rough guess at the equivalent yield:

$$\frac{£38,865 \times 0.827}{2.649} = £12,148$$

Thus the equivalent yield is

$$\frac{£5,000 + £12,148}{£246,835} = 6.94\%$$

The annual equivalent can then be recalculated using this yield in an iterative approach (constant repetition) until the two rates equate.

The approach can be seen graphically as follows.

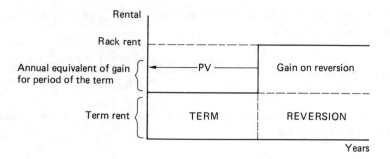

$$\text{Initial yield generally} = \frac{\text{income}}{\text{capital value}}$$

In this case:

$$\text{equivalent yield} = \frac{\text{term rent} + \text{annual equivalent of gain}}{\text{price}}$$

The calculation takes the capital value of the gain on reversion back to year 0 and then annualises it for the period of the term. This gives the rental value for the period which, when added to the term rent, gives an equivalent overall rent to be used in the calculation of the yield.

Solution by Discounted Cash Flow:

Years	Cash flow	YP 3 years @ 6%	PV £1 in 3 years @ 6%	PV
1–3	5,000	2.673		13,365
3 on	285,700		0.8396	239,873
				253,238
		less price		246,835
		NPV		+6,403

Years	Cash flow	YP 3 years @ 7%	PV £1 in 3 years @ 7%	PV
1–3	5,000	2.624		13,120
3 on	285,700		0.8163	233,127
				246,337
		less price		246,835
		NPV		− 498

By linear interpolation:

$$\text{IRR} = 6\% + \frac{6,403}{6,403 + 498}$$

$$= 6\% + 0.93$$

The equivalent yield (IRR) = 6.93%.

Parry's Tables give a more accurate answer of 6.91%, as there are approximations in the above approaches. This approach is basically the same as calculating a Gross Redemption Yield on a fixed interest security which is redeemable at a future date (such as a dated Government stock).

Example 7.2

A shop premises in a provincial High Street was recently let for £20,000 per annum exclusive on a modern full repairing and insuring lease for 25 years with 5 year rent reviews. The freehold subject to the lease was subsequently sold for £275,000.

You have been asked by a client to value the freehold interest in a comparable shop nearby let on a full repairing and insuring lease for 25 years with 5 year reviews 2 years ago. The current rent is £15,000 p.a.

Freehold yield from comparable is

$$\frac{£20,000}{£275,000} \times 100\% = 7.27\%, \text{ say } 7\%$$

Traditional valuation:

Term, rent reserved	£15,000	
YP 3 yrs @ 6%	2.67	
		£40,050
Reversion to rack rent	£20,000	
YP in perp. @ 7% def. 3 yrs	11.66	
		£233,200
Capital value		£273,250

Solution by formula:

Gain on reversion = value on reversion − price
Value on reversion

Rack rent	£20,000	
YP in perp. @ 7%	14.285	
		£285,700

Gain on reversion = 285,800 − 273,250 = 12,550

$$\text{Annual equivalent of gain} = \frac{£12,550 \times \text{PV £1 @ say } 6\tfrac{1}{2}\% \text{ in 3 yrs}}{\text{YP 3 yrs @ say } 6\tfrac{1}{2}\%}$$

$$= \frac{£12,550 \times 0.828}{2.65} = £3,921$$

$$\text{Equivalent yield} = \frac{\text{term rent} + \text{annual equivalent of gain}}{\text{price}}$$

$$= \frac{£15,000 + £3,921}{£273,250} = 6.92\%$$

You can, for accuracy, recalculate the term rates at higher yields until term rates = equivalent yield.

Solution by DCF:

Years	Cash flow	YP @ 6%	PV @ 6%	PV	YP @ 7%	PV @ 7%	PV
1–3	15,000	2.6730	—	40,095	2.6243	—	39,364
3 on	285,700	—	0.8396	239,874	—	0.8163	233,217
		Present value		279,969			272,581
		less price		273,250			273,250
		NPV		6,719			−669

By linear interpolation:

$$\text{IRR (Equivalent yield)} = 6\% + \frac{6{,}719}{6{,}719 + 669} = 6.91\%$$

Equivalent yield valuation:

Term, rent reserved	£15,000	
YP 3 yrs @ 6.91%	2.63	
		£39,450
Reversion to rack rent	£20,000	
YP in perp. @ 6.91% def. 3 yrs	11.85	
		£237,000
Capital value		£276,450

Compared to traditional term and reversion:

Capital value	£273,250

GROSS REDEMPTION YIELDS

At the end of chapter 5 the various yields were discussed. As has been mentioned, the equivalent yield is the same as a Gross Redemption Yield on a Government security.

Example 7.3

Extract from the *Financial Times*, 10 July 1990:

British Funds
'Shorts' (Lives up to Five Years)

1990			Price £	+ or −	Yield	
High	Low	Stock			Int.	Red.
$96\frac{13}{32}$	$81\frac{31}{32}$	Treasury 10% Ln 1994	$93\frac{1}{16}$	...	10.75	12.34

This is Treasury stock giving a 10% yield on the nominal value of £100 and is being sold at £93 $\frac{1}{16}$. It is redeemable in 1994 at par (the nominal value of £100). The high and low prices are noted for the year to the left side and the *Financial Times* has calculated the initial yield (Int.) and the redemption yield (Red.).

The initial yield is found from the 10% return on the nominal value of £100 which generates an income of £10. Thus yield = income/capital value (price) = £10/£93.0625 = 10.75%.

The redemption yield can be calculated as follows. The investment is purchased for £93 $\frac{1}{16}$ and has a residual value of £100 at the end of its income life.

```
CAPITAL OUTLAY        £ 93.0625
TRIAL RATES                 12%        13%
CASH FLOWS:
Year 1                £    10
Year 2                £    10
Year 3                £    10
Year 4                £   110
```

Year	Cash flow	PV £1 @ 12%	Present Value
0	−93.0625	1	−93.0625
1	10	0.8929	8.9290
2	10	0.7972	7.9720
3	10	0.7118	7.1180
4	110	0.6355	69.9050
	NET PRESENT VALUE		0.8615

Year	Cash flow	PV £1 @ 13%	Present Value
0	−93.0625	1	−93.0625
1	10	0.8850	8.8850
2	10	0.7831	7.8310
3	10	0.6931	6.9310
4	110	0.6133	67.4630

NET PRESENT VALUE   −1.9525

$$IRR = R_1 + \left\{ (R_2 - R_1) \times \frac{NPV\ R_1}{NPV\ R_2 + NPV\ R_1} \right\}$$

$$R_1 = 12;\ NPV\ R_1 = 0.8615$$
$$R_2 = 13;\ NPV\ R_2 = 1.9525$$

$$IRR = 12.30\%$$

For index linked stock, the same approach can be taken. Note that these funds have an inflation allowance and are therefore real rates of interest without inflation and risk.

Example 7.4

Extract from the *Financial Times*, 10 July 1990:

British Funds
Index-Linked

1990 High	Low	Stock	Price £	+ or −	Yield (1)	(2)
108 $\frac{19}{32}$	103 $\frac{1}{4}$	Treasury 2% 1994	108	−1/8	4.11	4.77

(1) and (2) are the prospective redemption yields on a projected inflation of 10% and 5% respectively.

Treasury 2% stock means a £2 income on the nominal value of £100. If the inflation rate is 5% then 5% of the nominal value is added so that the income is £2 + £5 = £7.

The investment is purchased for £108 and has a residual value of £100 at the end of its income life.

CAPITAL OUTLAY　　　£　　108
TRIAL RATES　　　　　　　　4%　　　　5%
CASH FLOWS:
Year 1　　　　　　　　　£　　7
Year 2　　　　　　　　　£　　7
Year 3　　　　　　　　　£　　7
Year 4　　　　　　　　　£　　107

Year	Cash flow	PV £1 @ 4%	Present Value
0	−108	1	−108.0000
1	7	0.9615	6.7305
2	7	0.9246	6.4722
3	7	0.8890	6.2230
4	107	0.8548	91.4636

NET PRESENT VALUE　　　2.8893

Year	Cash flow	PV £1 @ 5%	Present Value
0	−108	1	−108.0000
1	7	0.9524	6.6668
2	7	0.9070	6.3490
3	7	0.8638	6.0466
4	107	0.8227	88.0289

NET PRESENT VALUE　　　−0.9087

$$IRR = R_1 + \left\{ (R_2 - R_1) \times \frac{NPV\ R_1}{NPV\ R_2 + NPV\ R_1} \right\}$$

$R_1 = 4;\ NPV\ R_1 = 2.8893$
$R_2 = 5;\ NPV\ R_2 = 0.9087$

IRR = 4.76%

Note that this is an approximate value because of the interpolation.

Undated stock can be analysed on the same basis, but this is a traditional initial yield without any redemption. From the *Financial Times*, we can find the entry for the Consolidated Stock (the National Debt) which has no redemption date, quoted.

Example 7.5

Extract from the *Financial Times*, 10 July 1990:

British Funds
Index-Linked

1990			Price	+ or −	Yield	
High	Low	Stock	£		Int.	Red.
$41\frac{3}{32}$	$33\frac{9}{16}$	Consols 4 pc	$35\frac{1}{4}$	$+\frac{5}{16}$	11.35	—

The income of 4% on the nominal value of £100 is £4. The yield is income/price = £4/£35.25 = 11.35%.

8 Equated Rents

Equated rents are sometimes called 'constant rents'. In order to avoid confusion and to relate to other chapters of the book, the term 'equated rents' will be used here.

There is a problem of adjusting rents payable in respect of a lease with non-standard rent review patterns. If most comparable evidence is on the basis of 5 year reviews, how would you adjust the rentals for different review patterns? Of course there may be no problem if there were to be no inflation – rents may remain relatively constant and longer review patterns would not be disadvantageous. Some would hold this view to be dangerous; over a period of time even without inflation, factors may change in such a way that higher rents could be obtained. Such factors could include an increase in the economic wealth of a country such that there is more consumer expenditure, retail profits increase, increased demand for shop premises and a willingness to pay higher rents. A new property development could establish itself along with its profitability, or new tenants could establish a pattern of trade after moving into a certain location; comparable evidence will rely on other successful outlets in the area. Of course, if there is a decline in favourable conditions then a longer rent review period may be beneficial to the landlord. Thus, without inflation, the effect of a longer rent review period is lessened; however there is an element of risk to both sides in being drawn into a long review situation. If inflation is allowed for as the normal economic situation, as has been evident since the late 1950s, then it must be in the landlords' interest to introduce shorter review periods. For the tenant this is obviously disadvantageous. However, although increasing change in the economic environment must increase uncertainty for business operations, shorter review periods, when combined with shorter leases and possible breaks in the lease where the tenant can terminate it early, may be advantageous to the tenant.

The method of calculating equated rents assumes rental growth, otherwise there would be no difference in value between, say, 3 year rent reviews and 7 year reviews. The assumption of growth is built into most valuations where initial yields are so low (see chapter 5 on Equated Yields).

An approach to deal with this problem are the *Tables of Constant Rent* devised by Jack Rose. His calculations involve the factor K (the *Constant Rent Factor*) which when applied to the rent payable for a normal review pattern will produce the required enhanced rental payable on a longer review pattern or the lesser rent on a shorter review pattern. The general pattern of review in the UK is on a 5 year basis, but this will depend on the type, nature, location of the property and the covenant of the tenant. The actual pattern does not matter too much but the norm for the rent review periods, whether this be 3, 5, 7 years or any other period, will provide the rental comparables which need to be adjusted if the rent review pattern under negotiation differs from this norm and thus the comparables.

K is based on the formula:

$$K = \frac{A-B}{A-1} \times \frac{C-1}{C-D}$$

where:

A is the amount of £1 @ $R\%$ (the equated yield) for L years (the actual abnormal review period)
B is the amount of £1 @ $G\%$ (the growth rate for property of this type) for L years
C is the amount of £1 @ $R\%$ for Z years (normal rent review pattern)
D is the amount of £1 @ $G\%$ for Z years

This appears complicated at first sight, but it is really a question of accurate use of the tables and a calculator. Note that L (the abnormal rent review period) and Z (the normal rent review period) will be known for the lease of the subject property and from knowledge of normal leases granted. G may be known from research carried out and published, and approaches to the calculation of the growth rate have been considered in chapter 5. The same remarks apply to the equated yield: this could be the established yield on the basis of market evidence or the required target yield of a particular client.

Before giving an example of the above method it should be noted that the same results can be obtained from *Donaldson's Tables* of the equated yield. We are already aware of the relationship between yields, rental levels and capital values, thus:

$$\text{initial yield} = \frac{\text{rack rent}}{\text{capital value}}$$

In *Donaldson's Tables* there are four variables: the equated yield, the growth rate, the review pattern and the initial yield. If, as assumed with *Rose's Tables*, we assume that the equated yield and growth rate are known or estimated, and the review period is known from the lease, then the initial yield can be calculated. It would thus be possible to calculate initial yields for the normal and abnormal rent review period. The purpose of the exercise is to ensure that the capital value of the investment remains the same for the client by increasing rent on a long review and vice versa.

From the relationship:

$$\text{initial yield} = \frac{\text{rack rent}}{\text{capital value}}$$

if capital values are the same then rents must vary in proportion to the initial yields. This is in fact the basis of Rose's constant K. The constant rent factor is the ratio between the initial yield calculated on the abnormal review to the initial yield in the normal review. The basis of this approach is explained below and brings together the two approaches of constant and equated rents.

ROSE'S TABLES

Rose in the tables is finding a constant which when multiplied by the normal rent (that is, one based on a 5 year rent review pattern) will provide the abnormal rent payable which is equivalent (one which will maintain the capital value of the investment at the same level as a normal review pattern). Thus

$$\text{Income}^A = K \times \text{Income}^N$$

so

$$\frac{\text{Income}^A}{\text{Income}^N} = K$$

where:

Income^N is the net income obtained under a normal rent review pattern
Income^A is the net income obtained under an abnormal rent review pattern
K is the constant rent factor.

DONALDSON'S TABLES

As has been mentioned, *Donaldson's Tables* can provide initial yields for various rent review patterns if we know the other three variables – the rent review pattern, the equated yield and the growth rate.

Let the initial yield on normal review be I^N and the initial yield on abnormal review patterns I^A. So

$$I^A = \frac{\text{Income}^A}{CV^A} \quad \text{and} \quad I^N = \frac{\text{Income}^N}{CV^N}$$

where CV^N and CV^A are the capital values on normal and abnormal rent reviews.

However, the purpose of the exercise is to adjust the rents for different review patterns so that the investor still has the same capital value, so we want $CV^A = CV^N$. Hence

$$I^A = \frac{\text{Income}^A}{CV^A} = I^N = \frac{\text{Income}^N}{CV^N}$$

$$\frac{\text{Income}^A}{\text{Income}^N} = \frac{I^A}{I^N} = K \text{ (see above)}$$

so K can be obtained from the ratio of the initial yields from the tables.

The following example calculates the constant rent factor and applies it using Rose's equation.

Example 8.1

Calculate the rent appropriate on rent review for a lease with 21 year rent reviews. The lessor's required return on capital is 15% (equated yield) and the growth rate anticipated is 8%. The rack rent is £10,000 p.a. on a normal review pattern of 5 years.

$$K = \frac{\text{Amount of £1 @ 15\% for 21 years} - \text{Amount of £1 @ 8\% for 21 years}}{\text{Amount of £1 @ 15\% for 21 years} - 1} \times$$

$$\frac{\text{Amount of £1 @ 15\% for 5 years} - 1}{\text{Amount of £1 @ 15\% for 5 years} - \text{Amount of £1 @ 8\% for 5 years}}$$

$$= \frac{18.8215 - 5.0338}{18.8215 - 1} \times \frac{2.0114 - 1}{2.0114 - 1.4693}$$

$$= 1.443$$

Thus the rent appropriate on review is

$K \times$ rent on normal review $= 1.443 \times$ £10,000 p.a. $=$ £14,430 p.a.

This answer could be found by a number of additional methods:

(1) From *Rose's Tables* which use the above formula.

(ii) From *Donaldson's Tables* using the ratio of initial yields on normal and abnormal reviews already mentioned.

(iii) By the same approach as outlined in (ii) but using the underlying formula as indicated in chapter 5:

$$I = E - E \left\{ \frac{(1 + G)^n - 1}{(1 + E)^n - 1} \right\}$$

where: $E =$ equated yield
$G =$ growth rate
$n =$ rent review period
$I =$ initial yield.

Note that I^A and I^N are calculated and the ratio taken to find K, as mentioned before.

Example 8.2

The rack rent of an investment with 5 year rent reviews is £10,000 p.a. Your client wants a 10% return (equated yield) and the growth rate of the investment is 8%. The subject lease has rent review of 21 years. What rent should be charged on review?

(i) Using Rose's formula:

$$K = \frac{\text{Amount of £1 @ 10\% for 21 years} - \text{Amount of £1 @ 8\% for 21 years}}{\text{Amount of £1 @ 10\% for 21 years} - 1} \times$$

$$\frac{\text{Amount of £1 @ 10\% for 5 years} - 1}{\text{Amount of £1 @ 10\% for 5 years} - \text{Amount of £1 @ 8\% for 5 years}}$$

$$= \frac{7.4002 - 5.0338}{7.4002 - 1} \times \frac{1.6105 - 1}{1.6105 - 1.4693}$$

$$= 1.598$$

Thus the rent appropriate on review is

K × rent on normal review = 1.598 × £10,000 p.a. = £15,980 p.a.

(ii) Using *Rose's Tables:*
Rose uses a different terminology in his tables: the rent review pattern and the growth rates are as already used, but the equated yield is termed the 'nominal risk rate required'. There are tables of nominal risk rate for each rate which are subdivided for levels of growth rate. The appropriate initial yield or real rate is taken for the rent review periods concerned and the ratio calculated. The table we require here is for the equated yield at 10% and the table is laid out thus:

NOMINAL RISK RATE REQUIRED 10%

Anticipated Growth Rate %	Rent review periods (Years)					
	3	5	7	10	14	21
2						
$2\frac{1}{2}$						
3						
$3\frac{1}{2}$						
4						
$4\frac{1}{2}$						
5						
$5\frac{1}{2}$						
6						
$6\frac{1}{2}$						
7						
$7\frac{1}{2}$						
8	2.15372	2.31253	2.47590	2.72829	3.07527	3.69738
9						
10						

Only the required line is filled in. Thus to find K we need to:

- Find the table for the appropriate nominal risk rate (the equated yield) here 10%
- Find the line for the appropriate growth rate (here 8%)
- Find the real risk rates (initial yields) for the appropriate rent reviews (5, 21 years).

K is the ratio of the abnormal review real risk rate to the normal =

$$\frac{3.69738}{2.31253} = 1.599$$

So rent on review is

$K \times$ rent on normal review = $1.599 \times £15,000 = £15,990$ p.a.

The difference in answer from (i) is due to rounding errors.

(iii) Using *Donaldson's Tables:*
These tables are arranged on the basis of a growth rate classification. Taking the appropriate growth rate, the table looks like this:

GROWTH RATE 8%

Review period				Alternative review periods				
5		3	7	10	14	21	25	33
Initial Yields	Equated Yields		Corresponding Initial Yields					
3	10.6	2.80	3.21	3.53	3.97	4.73	5.16	5.97
3.25	10.81							
3.5	11.03							
3.75	11.25							
⋮								
12								

The initial yields increase at a quarter per cent intervals to 12% along the left-hand column, representing the initial yields for the normal review pattern (5 years). The equated yield column is next and then the initial yields corresponding to the appropriate alternative review periods.
   Thus the approach is:

(1) Look up the appropriate growth rate page (8%).
(2) Look down the equated yield column to find 10%. The nearest is 10.6 as the initial yields do not start until 3% for the 5 year review period, thus, for accuracy, this will need to be calculated from the formula (see next section). As a rough guide, we will use the line of initial yield corresponding to the equated yield = 10.6.

(3) Find initial yield for 5 year reviews (3%) and for 21 year reviews (4.73%) in the same line where the equated yield = 10.6. Thus:

$$\frac{\text{Initial yield on 21 year reviews}}{\text{Initial yield on 5 year reviews}} = \frac{I^A}{I^N} = K \text{ (see above)}$$

$$K = \frac{4.73}{3} = 1.577 \text{ so rent approximation is £15,770 p.a.}$$

Linear interpolation of the tables gives $I^A = 3.62\%$ and $I^N = 2.25\%$, thus giving an approximation of $K = 1.609$ with a rent approximation of £16,090.

(iv) Using the equation underlying *Donaldson's Tables:*

$$I = E - E \left\{ \frac{(1+G)^n - 1}{(1+E)^n - 1} \right\} \text{ (Note that all rates are expressed as decimals)}$$

where E = equated yield
G = growth rate
n = rent review period
I = initial yield.

Here $E = 0.10$ and $G = 0.08$. We then work out the initial yields for the abnormal and normal review pattern.

For 21 year reviews:

$$I^A = 0.10 - 0.10 \left\{ \frac{(1 + 0.08)^{21} - 1}{(1 + 0.10)^{21} - 1} \right\} = 0.0370$$

For 5 year reviews:

$$I^N = 0.10 - 0.10 \left\{ \frac{(1 + 0.08)^5 - 1}{(1 + 0.10)^5 - 1} \right\} = 0.0231$$

$$\frac{\text{Initial yield on 21 year reviews}}{\text{Initial yield on 5 year reviews}} = \frac{I^A}{I^N} = K \text{ (see above)}$$

$$K = \frac{0.370}{0.231} = 1.601$$

so rent is £16,010 p.a.

A FLOWCHART THROUGH ABNORMAL RENT REVIEWS

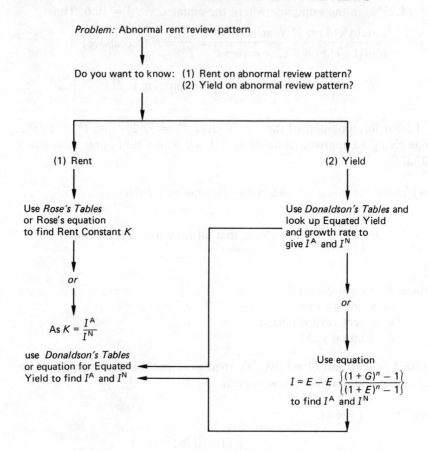

Problem: Abnormal rent review pattern

Do you want to know: (1) Rent on abnormal review pattern?
(2) Yield on abnormal review pattern?

(1) Rent

(2) Yield

Use *Rose's Tables*
or Rose's equation
to find Rent Constant K

Use *Donaldson's Tables* and
look up Equated Yield
and growth rate to
give I^A and I^N

or

or

As $K = \dfrac{I^A}{I^N}$

use *Donaldson's Tables*
or equation for Equated
Yield to find I^A and I^N

Use equation

$$I = E - E \left\{ \frac{(1+G)^n - 1}{(1+E)^n - 1} \right\}$$

to find I^A and I^N

9 Rent Payments

In the traditional method of valuation (chapter 2) it was seen that the basis of capitalisation of the rent is that the income is received annually in arrears. This has nothing to do with any inherent weaknesses of the method but comes about because, conventionally, valuation tables were based on interest compounded annually. The compound interest formula is:

$$(1 + i)^n$$

When interest is paid more frequently than once a year, then the formula is modified to become:

$$\left(1 + \frac{i}{m}\right)^{nm}$$

where i = rate of interest (%)
n = number of years
m = number of payments per year.

The more frequently interest is paid, the greater will be the amount earned.

Example 9.1

£1,000 invested at 8% compound for 4 years will amount to:

£1,000 × $(1 + i)^n$

= £1,000 × $(1 + 0.08)^4$ = £1,360

Using *Parry's Tables:*

Sum invested £1,000
Amount of £1 in 4 yrs @ 8%   1.360
_____

£1,360

If the interest is to be paid every six months, the resulting amount would be:

$$£1,000 \times \left(1 + \frac{0.08}{2}\right)^{4\times2} = £1,000 \times (1.04)^8 = £1,368.6$$

And if interest is paid quarterly:

$$£1,000 \times \left(1 + \frac{0.08}{4}\right)^{4\times4} = £1,000 \times (1.02)^{16} = £1,372.8$$

Though Parry's Amount of £1 Table is compounded annually, it is possible to use it if the 'years' are regarded as the number of period payments:

Sum invested	£1,000
Amount of £1 in 16 'years' @ 2%	1.3728
	£1,372.8

Should the interest payment only be required, then the formula is simply modified again:

$$(1 + i)^n - 1$$

which for the above annual example becomes:

$$(1 + 0.8)^4 - 1 = 0.36$$

the amount of interest being £1,000 × 0.36 = £360.

And quarterly:

$$(1 + 0.2)^{16} - 1 = 0.3728$$

As pointed out in chapter 1, for discounting purposes the formulae are inverted and therefore become:

$$\text{Present Value of } £1 = \frac{1}{(1 + i)^n}$$

$$\text{Present Value of } £1 \text{ (interest paid } m \text{ times per annum)} = \frac{1}{\left(1 + \dfrac{i}{n}\right)^{nm}}$$

The importance of this for valuation purposes is that when using the conventional tables, the assumption must be that the rent is received annually in arrears, whereas modern leases usually require the rent to be paid quarterly in advance. Income being capitalised is affected not only by the increased frequency of payment, as just illustrated, but also as explained in the concept of discounting (chapter 3) – an income to be received now is worth more than one to be received in the future. So, once again, the formula must be modified.

Modification of the Year's Purchase for n years is simply that one period of income will be received now, leaving $(n-1)$ periods remaining. This can be expressed as:

YP in advance for n periods $= 1 +$ YP in arrear $(n - 1)$ periods

For example, for annually in advance:

YP in advance 10 years @ 8% $= 1 +$ YP in arrear $(10-1)$ years @ 8%
$= 1 +$ YP in arrear 9 years @ 8%
$= 1 + 6.2469$
$= 7.2469$

The affect on capitalisation will again be obvious, assuming an income of £1,000 per annum:

Net income	£1,000	
YP 10 years in arrear @ 8%	6.71	
	———	
		£6,710

Net income	£1,000	
YP 10 years in advance @ 8%	7.2469	
	———	
		£7,247

The difference will not be as great when rent is paid quarterly:

Net income	£250	
YP 10 years quarterly in arrear @ 2% per quarter	27.3555	
(YP 40 'years' @ 2%)	———	
		£6,839

Net income	£250	
YP 10 years quarterly in advance @ 2%	27.9026	
(1 + YP 39 'years' @ 2%)	———	
		£6,976

A difficulty arises when deciding on the quarterly interest rate to be used. It was shown above that where interest is paid more frequently than annually, then the resulting return is higher. If interest @ 2% is paid quarterly, the annual rate becomes:

$$(1 + 0.2)^4 - 1 = 0.0824 = 8.24\%$$

This means that the income will have been undervalued using a quarterly yield of 2%. If the nominal annual rate is to be 8%, then the quarterly rate can be calculated from:

$$(1 + x)^4 = (1 + 0.08)^1$$
$$x = \sqrt[4]{(1.08)} - 1$$
$$x = 0.0194$$
$$\text{Quarterly rate} = 1.94\%$$

The Year's Purchase can be calculated from the formula:

$$\frac{1 - PV}{i} = \frac{1 - [1/(1 + i)^n]}{i} \text{ (see chapter 1 and its appendix)}$$

Note:

$$\frac{1}{(1 + i)^n} = (1 + i)^{-n}$$

therefore:

YP for n years $= \dfrac{1 - (1 + i)^{-n}}{i}$

Therefore at 1.94% for 39 'years':

$$\text{YP 39 'years'} = \frac{1 - (1 + 0.0194)^{-39}}{0.0194}$$

$$= 27.1819$$

YP quarterly in advance 10 years @ 8% equals:

$$1 + 27.1819 = 28.1819$$

Valuing the quarterly income:

Quarterly income	£250
YP quarterly in adv. 10 years @ 8%	28.1819
	£7,045

Using the former *Parry's Tables* required modification to value quarterly in advance investments, but the latest edition includes Quarterly in Advance Tables, so the calculation is now simplified to:

$$
\begin{array}{lr}
\text{Annual income} & \text{£1,000} \\
\text{YP Quarterly in Advance 10 yrs @ 8\%} & 7.0424 \\
\hline
& \text{£7,042}
\end{array}
$$

Tables for Dual Rate quarterly in advance adjusted for tax are also available for valuing leasehold profit rents, as dealt with in chapter 10.

Whether valuation is made in advance or in arrears, it is important for the valuer to know the date of completion of sale, which is unlikely to be when rent payment is due. 'In advance' means that a period payment is to be received immediately; should this not be the case, then the income pattern is effectively received in arrears.

Recognition of the rent income pattern is essential for analysis so that the correct discount rate is used for the income pattern being valued; the investor may have a different view of an acceptable rate for in advance and in arrear incomes received quarterly or annually.

10 Taxation

CONVENTIONAL APPROACH

Using the conventional method of property valuation, the view is taken that the income from the investment will be treated for income or corporation tax purposes in the same way as any other source of income; for example, income from Government stock is paid 'gross of tax' in the same way that rent is received by the investor. Incomes from investments, whether from stock, securities or different types of property, will be capitalised using the appropriate Year's Purchase for the rate of interest, reflecting the investment's security. By deducting tax at the standard rate from the incomes, the relative position of each investment will not be altered so for this reason the conventional view is taken that tax need not be deducted as an outgoing from rent before capitalisation. Furthermore, as the tax position of investors can vary widely, nothing is gained when valuing for sale on the open market by deducting tax at an assumed rate.

Where interest is paid 'net of tax', the rate of interest must be 'grossed up' using the gross tax factor for the standard rate of tax. So that when a Building Society quotes an investment rate of '12% – gross equivalent of 16% for tax payers at 25%' this is arrived at by:

Investment rate	0.12
Gross Tax Factor @ 25%	1.333
Gross Equivalent Investment Rate	0.16

Tax adjustment factors can be found in *Parry's Tables*, 11th edition, page 329.

If two investments are to be compared, one being quoted at a yield of 10% gross of tax, the other at 8% net of tax, it is necessary for the yields to be on the same basis. Assuming tax at standard rate:

Gross of tax yield	10.00
Net tax factor @ 25%	0.75 (1 − tax rate)
Net of tax yield	7.5%

from which it can be seen the net yield quoted will give a higher return.
Alternatively, the net of tax yield can be converted to gross by:

Net of tax yield	8.00
Gross tax factor @ 25%	1.333 $(1/(1 - \text{tax rate}))$
Gross of tax yield	10.66%

giving, of course, the same conclusion.

LEASEHOLD INTERESTS

A fundamental factor considered by an investor is that the capital sum invested will be returned. In the case of freehold interests which last in perpetuity, that is, the income is infinite, the capital can be recovered at any time by selling the interest.

Where the income to be valued is terminable, that is, the income is finite, as is the case with leasehold interests, the conventional view is that an annual sinking fund should be established to replace the capital sum invested on termination of the interest. Such funds are in the form of an insurance policy maturing on expiry of the interest, the annual premium required being found from the income received; this is allowed for by capitalising the profit rent from the investment using Dual Rate YP factor.

It is imperative that an annual sinking fund investment should not fail otherwise the capital will not be returned; such 'riskless' investments will have a low yield – typically about 5%. However low the income generated by the investment it is still a source of income subject to income tax which effectively reduces the yield from the policy, so the rate of interest must be 'netted down' to find the effective yield, as illustrated above. As a further example for a tax being paid at 40%:

Policy rate of interest	5.00%
Net tax factor 40%	0.6
Effective yield	3.00%

Certain expenses may be incurred by an investor holding an interest in real property – for example, repairs and reinstatement insurance – which can be deducted from rental income before tax is assessed. An annual sinking fund premium is not such an allowable expense; in other words, the premium is subject to tax. However, if the premium is reduced by tax it will be insufficient to replace the capital sum, therefore it is necessary to 'gross up' the premium to an amount which after tax will leave the required premium.

Valuation of leasehold interests are conventionally valued using Dual Rate Year's Purchase Tables adjusted for tax. The following example was used to illustrate this in chapter 2:

Net rental value	£15,000
Net rent paid	8,000
Profit rent	7,000
YP 4 yrs @ 9% & 3% (tax 40%)	2.048
Estimated capital value	£14,336

That the required return was 9% was further demonstrated by:

	Profit rent		£7,000
Less	Annual sinking fund:		
	Capital to be replaced	£14,336	
	ASF 4 yrs @ 3%	0.239	
	Annual sinking fund	3,426	
	Gross Tax factor @ 40%	1.667	
	Total allowance for ASF		5,711
	Remaining income		£1,289

$$\text{Return on capital } \frac{£1,289}{£14,336} \times 100 = 9\%$$

The allowance of £5,711 for the annual sinking fund includes the tax to be paid. This can be seen by:

	Sum allowed		£5,711
Less	Income tax @ 40% on	£5,711	
		0.4	2.284
	Amount remaining for ASF premium		£3,427

It can be seen that when valuing leasehold interests using the conventional method, income tax has two effects:

1. The rate of interest earned on the ASF policy is reduced.
2. The annual premium for the policy is subject to tax.

As the term of years lengthens, the affect of taxation on the premium reduces because of the discounting factor. This can be seen by studying the YP factors:

YP 4 years @ 9% & 3%   3.039
YP 4 years @ 9% & 3% (tax 40%)   2.048
Affect of tax: 33% reduction

YP 60 years @ 9% & 3%   10.402
YP 60 years @ 9% & 3% (tax 40%)   9.978
Affect of tax: 4% reduction

NON-TAX PAYERS

Investors who are not subject to income tax, such as pension funds, are placed in a particularly advantageous position compared with tax-paying investors when purchasing leasehold interests, because obviously neither the sinking fund rate nor the annual premium is reduced. In the case of the above example, a non-tax payer valuation would be:

Profit rent   £7,000
YP 4 yrs @ 9% & 5%   3.106
_____

Value   £21,742

which is over 50% more than the tax payer's value.

NET OF TAX VALUATIONS – FREEHOLD INTERESTS

As the conventional method generally disregards tax on income, analysis of sales will normally be on the same gross of tax basis.

Example 10.1

A freehold property recently let at the net rack rent of £8,000 has just been sold for £100,000. The yield will be:

$$\frac{8,000}{100,000} \times 100 = 8\%$$

This yield represents what the investment market is prepared to accept for a gross of tax income of £8,000.

If a net of tax analysis is required, the tax paid by the investor must be deducted from the income. Assuming tax at 40% this will be:

Gross of tax income	£8,000
Less tax @ 40%	3,200
Net income	4,800

$$\text{Yield } \frac{4,800}{100,000} \times 100 = 4.8\%$$

On this basis, a valuation must be made by capitalising the net of tax income using a net of tax yield:

Net of tax income	£4,800
YP in perp. @ 4.8%	20.833
Capital value	£100,000

A net of tax valuation will only be required for an investor whose tax liability is known. It will be seen that a net of tax analysis of an interest let at rack rent will produce the same rate as one on a gross basis. However, this is not the case where there is rent below rack rent for a term of years.

Example 10.2

Value a freehold income or £750 per annum to be received for 5 years then reverting to rack rent of £1,000. For simplicity, a yield of 10% is used for term and reversion.

Gross of tax:

Rent	£ 750		
YP 5 yrs @ 10%	3.791		
		2,843	

Rack rent	£1,000		
YP perp. @ 10%	10.00		
PV £1 in 5 yrs @ 10%	0.621	6.21	
		6,210	
Capital value			£9,053

Net of tax

Rent	£ 750		
Less tax @ 40%	300		
Net of tax income	450		
YP 5 yrs @ 6%	4.212		
		1,895	

Rack rent	1,000		
Less tax @ 40%	400		
Net of tax income	600		
YP perp. @ 6%	16.667		
PV £1 in 5 yrs @ 6%	0.747	12.45	7,470
Capital Value			£9,365

NET OF TAX VALUATIONS – LEASEHOLD INTERESTS

The position regarding leasehold interests is the same as for freehold, namely the same result will be obtained for gross and net of tax basis where there is a single profit rent. When valuing net of tax though, it is not necessary to use tax adjusted Dual Rate YP tables because the total income tax liability will be deducted before capitalisation.

Example 10.3

Value on a gross and net basis a profit rent of £1,000 to be received for 5 years on which a yield of 10% is required with a sinking fund of 3%, the tax rate being 40%.

Gross of tax:

Profit rent	£1,000	
YP 5 yrs @ 10% & 3% (tax 40%)	2.416	
Value		£2,416

Net of tax

Profit rent	£1,000	
Less tax @ 40%	400	
Net of tax income	600	
YP 5 yrs @ 6% & 3%	4.027	
Capital Value		£2,416

There will be difference between gross and net of tax values where there is a term and reversion.

Example 10.4

Value on a gross and net basis a profit rent of £750 to be received for 5 years followed by a profit rent of £1,000 for a further 5 years with the same conditions as before.

Gross of tax:

Profit rent	£ 750		
YP 5 yrs @ 10% & 3% (tax 40%)	2.416		
			1,812
Profit rent	1000		
YP 5 yrs @ 10% & 3% (tax 40%) 2.416			
PV £1 in 5 yrs @ 10%	0.6209	1.5	1,500
Value			£3,312

Net of tax

Profit rent	£ 750	
Less tax @ 40%	300	
	——	
Net of tax income	450	
YP 5 yrs @ 6% & 3%	4.027	
	——	
		1,812

Profit rent		1,000	
Less tax at 40%		400	
Net of tax income		600	
YP 5 yrs @ 6% & 3%	4.027		
PV £1 in 5 yrs @ 6%	0.747	3.01	
	——	——	
			1,806
Capital value			——
			£3,618

Generally, valuers hold the conventional view that the property market consists of such a wide variety of investors, each having their own tax liability and strategies, there is little point in taking tax into consideration for open market valuation purposes. With regard to analysis, however, taxation is of great importance.

11 Risk

Risk is related to return – the level of risk determines the level of return. The Capital Market Line identified in chapter 4 shows this relationship.

Some texts differentiate between 'risk' and 'uncertainty'. It is considered that one can assess the risk in terms of probability as an actuary could assess insurance risk. Uncertainty is considered as being so unlikely that one cannot assess probability. In this book we have not differentiated between risk and uncertainty. The lack of certainty of return will lead to a discounting of future revenue.

Baum and Crosby (1988) have identified a number of possible risks which could affect a property investment, for instance:

1. Tenant risk
2. Sector risk
3. Structural risk
4. Legislation risk
5. Taxation risk
6. Planning risk
7. Legal risk.

Baum and Crosby also identify the difference between money risk and real risk. They define 'money risk' as the variation in money income, and 'real risk' as the variation in real income. Examples of differing investments which are affected by real and monetary risks are as follows

Risk	Real	Monetary
Low	Index linked Gilts	Fixed interest Gilts
↓	Equities	Bank deposits
	Property	Index linked gilts
High	Bank deposits	Property
	Fixed interest Gilts	Equities

Risk also needs to be distinguished between individual property investments and a portfolio of properties. Markowitz (1959) developed a basic portfolio model for risk attaching to a portfolio of investments, and this can be applied to investment properties. Markowitz showed that the risk is reduced in a portfolio by combining assets whose returns demonstrated less than perfect positive correlation. However there are two types of risk that will attach themselves to property under the analysis. The risks are called 'systematic' and 'unsystematic' risks, and these will be explained later in the development of this portfolio model. Unsystematic risks can be diversified away in a portfolio of property investments but systematic risks cannot. The effect of a balance portfolio construction is thus to reduce, but not abolish, property investment risk.

If we return to our analysis of the construction of market interest rates (see chapter 4) we find that the market interest rate is made up of three elements: a time-preference element, an inflation premium and a risk premium.

The accurate equation is:

$$I = (1 + i)(1 + d)(1 + r) - 1$$
(compare this equation with the one in chapter 4).

where I is the market interest rate
i is the time preference allowance
d is the inflation premium
r is the risk premium.

A risk-free return (RFR) thus equals

$$(1 + i)(1 + d) - 1$$

and

$$I = (1 + \text{RFR})(1 + r) - 1$$

so multiplying out we have

$$I = 1 + r + \text{RFR} + r\text{RFR} - 1$$

As rRFR will be small, an approximation of the above is $I = \text{RFR} + r$, so that the market rate of interest will be equal to a risk-free interest rate plus the risk premium.

THE THEORY OF RISK AND ITS APPLICATION TO PROPERTY INVESTMENT

There are two approaches to the inclusion of risk in a discounted cash flow method to property investments:

1. *Risk adjusted discount rate approach*. Here it is assumed that the cash flows are fixed and a risk element is incorporated into the discount rate.
2. *Risk adjusted cash flows*. A risk element is incorporated in the cash flow profile and the discount is made using a risk-free discount rate.

The traditional approach gives us the formula for discounting as the inverse of the Amount of £1 formulation; so Amount of £1 = $(1 + i)^n$ and Present Value is $1/(1 + i)^n$. Thus a £1 cash flow discounted back to the present at an interest rate of i (in decimals) is represented by this formulation. If the cash flow was £X then:

$$PV = X/(1 + i)^n$$

A discounted cash flow is the summation of a series of cash flows over a number of years (say n years), thus:

$$PV \text{ (over length of investment or project)} = \sum_{n=1}^{n=h} \frac{CF_n}{(1 + r_A)^n}$$

where PV is the Present Value of the discounted value of the project, CF_n is the residual cash flow to the equity investor, h is the holding period of the asset and r_A is the required rate of return (the discount rate).

As has been said above, the problems of applying the DCF techniques in practice relate to the estimation of the cash flows and applying the appropriate rate of return for the particular investor or client (see also chapter 2).

RISK ADJUSTED DISCOUNT RATE

In this analysis, no distinction is made between the Net Present Value approach and the Internal Rate of Return as investment selection criteria. In a constrained capital budgeting situation, the two criteria may lead to different investment decisions. This has been discussed in the chapter on NPV and IRR (chapter 3).

The rates of return used in the DCF calculation will depend on the specific requirements of the investor or client. The most important rate is the equity yield rate – the rate applying to the equity proportion of the investment excluding debt. Once the equity yield is specified, it is possible to estimate the present worth of the equity position. This rate can be based on the rate of return that suppliers of capital hope to receive for their capital. It is thus based on an opportunity cost principle; it is the rate foregone on the next best alternative investment opportunity.

The rate of return embodies the three factors of time preference, inflation premium and risk premium as mentioned above. Thus is summarised as:

$$I = \text{RFR} + r \text{ (risk premium)}$$

Note that we are using I as the required rate that an investor requires. In a perfect market this should accord with market rates, but this will depend on the personal requirements of the investor. We are thus using this calculation for analysis rather than valuation. Hence the risk-free rate here compensates for foregoing immediate consumption and provides a premium for inflation. This expectation of inflation is usually incorporated into the risk-free rate, but this is misleading as there is a risk of underestimating the level of future inflation and this additional risk will need to be incorporated into the risk premium. See above for the discussion on real and monetary risk.

The return required of a project can be taken from the Capital Asset Pricing Model. $I = \text{RFR} + r$ becomes more complex, r being broken down into two types of risk thus:

$$I = \text{RFR} + \beta(I_{\text{m}} - \text{RFR})$$

The first element of the risk premium is the risk premium for a project of average risk. This is $(I_{\text{m}} - \text{RFR})$, where I_{m} is the required rate of return for a project of average risk, so $I_{\text{m}} = \text{RFR} + r_{\text{m}}$, and thus r_{m} (the risk premium for a project of average risk) must be equal to $(I_{\text{m}} - \text{RFR})$.

The second element in the calculation is beta (β). This adjusts the mean risk for the relative riskiness of the project under consideration. This beta coefficient has been used in portfolio analysis for shares and defines the riskiness of the project as against the riskiness of investing in equity investments generally. It is possible to use data in the stock market to determine the mean risk premium, but this may need to be adjusted in a property situation to take into account the degree of equity and debt in a project (the gearing or leverage of a project), the type of project, the investment vehicle and the location. If the mean risk premium is, say, 5% on the market and the project is perceived as being twice as risky, then the risk premium is $2 \times 5\% = 10\%$. That is:

$$r \text{ (risk premium)} = \beta (I_{\text{m}} - \text{RFR})$$

and

$$I_m - \text{RFR} = 5\%, \beta = 2, \text{ so } r = 2\ (5\%)$$

The RFR is taken from index linked gilts which incorporate a time-preference element and an inflation allowance. Note, however, that the inflation premium is based on expectations of movements in inflation, and thus there may be some element of monetary risk in the yield at which they are sold.

To summarise, risk is of two kinds, systematic risk and unsystematic risk. The systematic risk is also called 'market risk' and relates to the change in returns to the project relative to the market in general. A beta of 2, as above, will mean that the project income will move 2% for each 1% move in the income average in the market; it is thus more volatile. Betas of ordinary shares on the Stock Market tend to range from 1.5 to 0.5. Unsystematic risk, also known as 'specific' or 'non-market risk', refers to factors specific to the project and is measured as a percentage return per annum; thus the higher the percentage, the higher the specific risk. A more traditional financial approach to risk is the consideration of the financial structure of a project, specifically its gearing. On the Stock Exchange, shares in companies with the highest betas tend to be highly geared and to come from highly cyclical industries. The same approach could be applied to the make-up of funding in a specific property project. Gearing is the ratio of debt capital to equity capital in any project, and thus high gearing means lots of loan and debt capital. In company financial structure, the definition is more exact and relates to the relationship between the funds provided to a company by its ordinary shareholders and the long-term sources of funds carrying a fixed interest charge or dividend (such as unsecured loans, debentures and preference shares). Thus the gearing ratio is:

$$\frac{\text{Long-term loans + preference shares}}{\text{Ordinary shareholders' funds}} \times 100\%$$

Companies and projects where profits are low or likely to fluctuate violently should not be too highly geared. Investors in such companies are running risks.

Thus, high gearing is risky but has a better effect on higher profitability projects than low earners. High gearing is more suitable for stable earners because there is more flexibility and ability to cope with fixed charges and obligations. Firms or projects with higher liquidity can cope more easily and lessen the risk of bankruptcy arising from higher gearing. Finally, higher gearing for a company or a project reduces the propensity to establish an unbroken dividend record, so there is a need to have an established dividend record to exploit high gearing. This is a basic summary of the effect of gearing on a property project; it is discussed more fully in chapter 15.

How the gearing effect can be incorporated into the beta analysis is shown in example 11.1.

Example 11.1

We assume that a property investment company has a value beta of 1.5 and that the capital structure is highly geared, say 90% debt and 10% equity finance. Since the debt is secure, the beta value is zero. The project beta value is a weighted average of the two types of capital, equity and debt finance. Thus:

$$\beta = (0) \times 0.90 + (1.50) \times 0.10 = 0.15$$

If the risk-free return is 10% and the mean equity return of the market is 20%, then:

$$I \text{ for project} = \text{RFR} + \beta (I_m - \text{RFR})$$
$$= 0.10 + 0.15 (0.20 - 0.10) = 0.115 = 11.5\%$$

RISK ADJUSTED CASH FLOWS

The expected value of any cash flow can be compared against a range of possibilities. If the expected value is x, then we can assess a range of possible values around this. We do this statistically by comparing the probable distribution around the expected level with a normal statistical distribution.

Thus the graph of the normal curve is compared against a probable curve in figure 11.1. The difference between the two outcomes can be examined statistically by way of the variance, which is the sum of the squares of the difference between the normal expected values and the probable distribution. It is the square of the standard deviation and is a measure of the variance to the expected outcome.

The use of this analysis is that probability can be built into the calculation. Say, for instance, that we are expecting profitability from a development to be £3 million, but it is possible that this may not be the precise outcome. Our analysis shows that with certain changes in the variables, the profit may be as low as £1 million and as high as £5 million. We can assign probabilities to the outcomes; that is, we could say that there is a 10% chance of the profit being as low as £1 million. By using the probabilities, we can plot the probable values and compare them stat-

Property Valuation Techniques

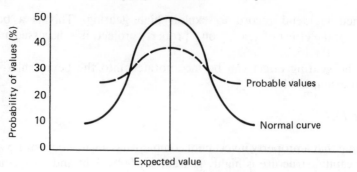

Figure 11.1

istically with a normal curve. Using this approach, we can be more precise statistically as to the outcome.

Example 11.2

Using the figures suggested above, we can assign probabilities to the outcome.

Possible values of outcome (V) £m	*Probability of occurrence* (P)
1	0.1
2	0.2
3	0.4
4	0.2
5	0.1
	TOTAL 1.0

Using the statistical approach above, we can consider our measure of missing the target as the standard deviation. To calculate the standard deviation, we work out the variance first. The standard deviation is the square root of the variance:

Standard deviation = σ (sigma)
Variance = σ^2

The variance is the sum of the squares of the deviation of the variable from the expected value. These deviations are weighted according to their probability. The expected values are:

Possible values (V) £m	Probability (P)	Weighted value (VP)
1	0.1	0.1
2	0.2	0.4
3	0.4	1.2
4	0.2	0.4
5	0.1	0.1
TOTAL	1.0	3.0

The sum of the weighted values $(\Sigma VP) = 3.0 =$ the expected value (EV). The variance $= \Sigma (V - EV)^2 \times P$, as discussed above. So:

Possible values (V) £m	Probability (P)	Deviation from expected value (3) (D)	Deviation² (D²)	Weighted probability (D²P)
1	0.1	−2	4	0.4
2	0.2	−1	1	0.2
3	0.4	0	0	0
4	0.2	1	1	0.2
5	0.1	2	4	0.4
TOTAL	1.0			1.2

Variance $= 1.2$.
Standard deviation $= \sqrt{1.2} = 1.095$.
Expected value $=$ £3 million.

By using a statistical analysis, the actual outcome can be compared against the expected outcome. Thus there is a 68% chance of the actual outcome being in the range of 1 standard deviation and a 95% chance of it being in a range of 2 standard deviations from the expected value. Thus

$$68\% \text{ chance of } V = EV \pm \sigma = \text{£3m} \pm \text{£1.095}$$
$$95\% \text{ chance of } V = EV \pm 2\sigma = \text{£3m} \pm \text{£2.19}$$

As the risk is now built into the cash flows, the discount rate applied to the level of the outcome would be the risk-free rate (say 10%, as example 11.1).

By using a Monte Carlo simulation, a valuation can be run a number of times by a computer to produce a range of results. The input range is picked at random but in accordance with the assigned probabilities to give a range of outputs which can then be plotted to provide the distribution curve (Byrne and Cadman, 1984).

REFERENCES

Baum, A. and Crosby, N. (1988). *Property Investment Appraisal*, Routledge and Kegan Paul, London.

Byrne, P. and Cadman, D. (1984). *Risk, Uncertainty and Decision Making in Property Development*, Spon. London.

Markowitz, H. (1959). *Portfolio Selection – Efficient Diversification of Investments*, Yale University Press, New Haven, Conn.

12 Problems of Leasehold Valuations

The leasehold interest is thought to be a less attractive investment than the freehold because the freeholder's consent is required for any proposed alteration to the property or disposal by assignment or sub-letting; also it is common practice for the leaseholder to meet all repairing and insuring obligations. In light of this, conventionally an addition of 0.5–1% is made to the freehold yield. Further, as the leasehold interest is a wasting asset it is considered that provision must be made for an annual sinking fund to replace the capital cost of the interest on expiry of the lease. Because the income from such a fund is subject to income tax, the already low rate of interest earned must be netted down and the annual sum must be increased to allow for the fund not being tax free. This results in the need to use a 'tax adjusted dual rate' YP factor to value leasehold interest.

A simple example will illustrate its use.

Example 12.1

An estimate is required of the value of the freehold interest in shop premises, in a secondary location where an 8% yield would be expected, and let at a net rent of £8,000 on a lease having 4 years remaining. The net rental value is estimated to be £15,000.

The valuation of the leasehold interest is:

Net rental value	£15,000	
Net rent paid	8,000	
Profit rent	7,000	
YP 4 yrs @ 9% & 3%/tax 40%	2.048	
Estimated capital value		£14,336

In this case, after adjusting the income to allow for the sinking fund element, increased to allow for tax, it can be seen that the initial yield is the

9% required:

Profit rent		£7,000
Less Annual sinking fund		
Capital to be replaced	£14,336	
ASF 4 yrs @ 3%	0.239	
	——————	
Annual sum	3,426	
Gross Tax factor @ 40%	1.667	
	——————	
Total allowance for ASF		5,711
		——————
Remaining income		£1,289
		——————

$$\text{Return on capital } \frac{£1,289}{£14,336} \times 100 = 9\%$$

A detailed explanation of the tax adjustments was given in chapter 10.

CRITIQUE OF SINKING FUND THEORY

It will be readily appreciated that there are a number of relatively 'riskless' investments producing a much higher annual return than 3% for lease-holder investors to use rather than the traditional insurance policy. However, most of these will have fluctuating interest rates and therefore, at each change of rate, the annual sum being invested will require adjustment.

A traditional sinking fund policy also will only replace the investment purchase price. On redemption, only the historic purchase price will be available for reinvestment, no provision having been made for inflationary effects on money. Therefore such a policy does not put a leasehold investment on the same basis as a freehold, the capital value of which will increase from the growth in rental value.

The continued use of providing for a sinking fund is that as the tax position of investors varies widely, it is the only way in which consistency, an essential tenet of valuation, can be maintained when estimating open market value.

TAXATION

Valuation of leasehold interests are conventionally valued using Dual Rate Year's Purchase Tables adjusted for tax. The following example was used to illustrate this in Chapter 1:

Net rental value	£15,000	
Net rent paid	8,000	
	———	
Profit rent	7,000	
YP 4 yrs @ 9% & 3% (tax 40%)	2.048	
	———	
Estimated capital value		£14,336
		———

That the required return of 9% was further demonstrated by:

Profit rent		£7,000	
Less Annual sinking fund			
Capital to be replaced	£14,336		
ASF 4 yrs @ 3%	0.239		
	———		
Annual sum	3,426		
Gross Tax factor @ 40%	1.667		
	———		
Total allowance for ASF		5,711	
		———	
Remaining income			£1,289
			———

$$\text{Return on capital } \frac{£1,289 \times 100}{£14,336} = 9\%$$

The allowance of £5,711 for the annual sinking fund includes the tax to be paid. This can be seen by:

Sum allowed		£5,711	
Less Income tax @ 40%	£5,711		
	0.4	2,284	
	———	———	
Amount remaining for ASF premium			£3,427
			———

It can be seen that when valuing leasehold interests using the conventional method, income tax has two effects:

1. The rate of interest earned on the ASF policy is reduced.
2. The annual premium for the policy is subject to tax.

Short leasehold interests

As the term of years lengthens, the effect of taxation on the premium reduces because of the discounting factor. This can be seen by studying the YP factors:

> YP 4 years @ 9% & 3%   3.039
> YP 4 years @ 9% & 3% (tax 40%)   2.048
> Effect of tax   33% reduction

> YP 60 years @ 9% & 3%   10.402
> YP 60 years @ 9% & 3% (tax 40%)   9.978
> Effect of tax   4% reduction

Non-tax payers

Investors who are not subject to income tax, such as pension funds, are placed in a particularly advantageous position compared with tax paying investors when purchasing leasehold interests, because obviously neither the sinking fund rate nor the annual premium is reduced. In the case of the above example, a non-tax payer valuation would be:

> Profit rent   £7,000
> YP 4 yrs @ 9% & 5%   3.106
> ─────
>
> Capital value   £21,742
> ─────────

which is over 50% more than the tax payer's value.

VARYING LEASEHOLD INCOMES

Consideration of leasehold interests which have varying incomes, where a rent below rack rent is received for a term of years, reveals a further difficulty with regard to the sinking fund concept.

Consider a leasehold interest of 15 years subject to an annual rent of £1,000 and sub-let with 4 years remaining at a rent of £2,000, the rack rental value being £3,000. Conventional valuation:

Term	Rent received	£2,000	
	Less rent paid	1,000	
	Profit rent	1,000	
	YP 4 yrs @ 9% & 3%	3.039	
			3,039
Reversion	Rental value	3,000	
	Less rent paid	1,000	
	Profit rent	2,000	
YP 11 yrs @ 10% & 3%		5.616	
PV £1 4 yrs @ 10%		0.683 3.836	
			7,672
	Capital value		£10,711

The assumption is that a sinking fund producing 3% per annum will be established to produce £10,711 in 15 years time:

Capital sum	£10,711
ASF 15 yrs @ 3%	0.0538
Annual sum to be invested	£576

Reconsider the valuation deducting the annual sinking fund amount:

$$
\begin{array}{lrr}
\text{Profit rent} & \text{£1,000} & \\
\textit{Less } \text{ASF} & 576 & \\
\cline{2-2}
\text{Net income} & 424 & \\
\text{YP 4 yrs @ 9\%} & 3.24 & \\
\cline{2-2}
& & 1,374
\end{array}
$$

$$
\begin{array}{lrr}
\text{Profit rent} & 2,000 & \\
\textit{Less } \text{ASF} & 576 & \\
\cline{2-2}
\text{Net income} & 1,424 & \\
\text{YP 11 yrs @ 10\%} \quad 6.495 & & \\
\text{PV £1 4 yrs @ 10\%} \quad 0.683 & 4.44 & \\
\cline{2-2}
& & 6,323 \\
\text{Value} & & \text{£7,697}
\end{array}
$$

It can be seen that the first valuation was overvalued. The reason for this is that a sinking fund has been provided for each income: the first to replace £3,039, the value of the term, and the second to replace £7,672, the value of the reversion. In other words, there has been a double sinking fund provided whereas only one sinking fund will be provided by a regular annual sum paid throughout the period of the lease.

The difficulty can be overcome by deducting the single annual sum required to replace the capital value from each stage of the valuation. This might seem difficult on the face of it because the capital value is what is required. The solution relies on the application of the time-honoured algebraic approach of letting x equal the unknown quantity. Reconsider the above problem:

Let x = capital value
The annual sum to replace this sum will be:

$$
\begin{array}{lr}
\text{Capital value} & \text{£}x \\
\text{ASF 15 yrs @ 3\%} & 0.0538 \\
\end{array}
$$

Annual sum to be deducted from rent income $0.0538x$

Term	Profit rent	£1,000	
	Less ASF	0.0538x	
	Net income	1,000 − 0.0538x	
	YP 4 yrs @ 9%	3.24	
	Value of term		3,240 − 0.1743x

Reversion	Profit rent	2,000	
	Less ASF	0.0538x	
	Net income	2,000 − 0.0538x	
YP 11 yrs @ 10%		6.495	
PV £1 4 yrs @ 10%		0.683	
		4.44	
	Value of reversion		8,880 − 0.2389x
	Capital value		12,120 − 0.4132x

As the capital value also = £x, a simple equation can be formed:

$$£x = 12,120 − 0.4132x$$
$$x + 0.4132x = 12,120$$
$$1.4132x = 12,120$$
$$x = \frac{12,120}{1.4132}$$

$$x = \text{Capital value} \quad £8,576$$

This can be checked as follows:

Calculate ASF	Capital	£8,576	
	ASF 15 yrs @ 3%	0.0538	
	ASF required		£461
Term	Profit rent	£1,000	
	Less ASF	461	
	Net rent	539	
	YP 4 yrs @ 9%	3.24	
			1,746
Reversion	Profit rent	2,000	
	Less ASF	461	
	Net income	1,539	
YP 11 yrs @ 10%	6.495		
PV £1 4 yrs @ 10%	0.683	4.44	
			6,833
	Value		£8,579 (rounding error)

It is an easy step to use the method for tax adjusted sinking funds. Using the same profit rent as before, but adjusted for income tax at 40%, calculate tax-adjusted ASF:

		Capital value £x
ASF 15 yrs @ 3%	0.0538	
Gross tax factor 40%	1.667	0.0897
	ASF	0.0897x

Term	Profit rent	£1,000
Less ASF 15 yrs @ 3% (tax 40%)		0.0897x

$$\text{Net income} \quad 1,000 - 0.0897x$$
$$\text{YP 4 yrs @ 9\%} \quad 3.24$$

$$3,240 - 0.291x$$

Reversion	Profit rent	2,000
Less ASF 15 yrs @ 3% (tax 40%)		0.0897x

$$\text{Net rent} \quad 2,000 - 0.0897x$$

YP 11 yrs @ 10%	6.495	
PV £1 4 yrs @ 10%	0.683	4.44

$$8,880 - 0.3983x$$

$$12,120 - 0.6893x$$

$$x = 12,120 - 0.6893x$$
$$x + 0.6893x = 12,120$$
$$x = \frac{12,120}{1.6893}$$
$$x = 7,175$$

This again can be checked as before:

Calculate ASF	Capital value	£7,175
	ASF 15 yrs @ 3% (tax 40%)	0.0897

$$644$$

Term		Profit rent	£1,000	
		Less ASF	644	
		Net income	356	
	YP 4 yrs @ 9%		3.24	
				1,153

Reversion		Profit rent	2,000	
		Less ASF	644	
			1,356	
YP 11 yrs @ 10%	6.495			
PV £1 4 yrs @ 10%	0.683		4.44	
				6,021

	Capital value		£7,174[*]

(* slight error due to rounding amounts)

13 Development Valuations and the Cash Flow Approach

Valuation of properties having development potential, whether green field sites or obsolete buildings, has long been undertaken by what is known as the Residual Method. The basis of this method is straightforward, namely:

Estimate of developed value	£x
Less Estimate of development costs	£y
(Residue) Value of site	£x − y

Development costs includes all the costs which will be incurred to complete the development, such as contractor's costs for buildings and road works, architect's fees, funding and the developer's profit. A simple example will illustrate the method.

Example 13.1

Four houses are to be built on a site fronting a road with all services. From comparable sales, the houses would sell at £100,000 each and take a year to build at a cost of £55,000 each. The cost of borrowing is 17% per annum.

Estimated development value 4 @ £100,000		£400,000
Development costs		
Building cost 4 @ £55,000	£220,000	
Architect's fees @ 10%	22,000	
Total borrowing	242,000	
Finance @ 17% for 6 months	20,570	
Agent's fees @ 2% of sale	8,000	
Developer's profit 15% of value	60,000	
Total costs		330,570
Total amount available for land acquisition		69,430

Total amount available for land acquisition	69,430
PV £1 @ 17% 1 year	0.855
Amount for acquisition	59,363
Less acquisition costs @ 3%	1,781
	57,582

Estimated development value of site £57,500

The sum available for land acquisition is as at the completion of the development and includes the cost of borrowing the amount for acquisition throughout the development period; thus this sum needs to be discounted back to the present day to find the acquisition price now. In acquiring the site legal, valuation and Stamp Duty fees will have to be paid; typically these are allowed at 3% or 4% of the discounted amount, though strictly this should be a percentage of the land price which is not yet known. So the result of the calculation is that the site should be purchased for £57,582 on which fees of £1,781 will be paid, giving a total amount of £59,363 to be borrowed at 17%. At the end of the development, this will amount to £69,430.

The method would be the same for a commercial development except that the developed value would be estimated by use of a simple investment valuation, the net income being capitalised by an appropriate Year's Purchase in perpetuity for a freehold development. In principle the approach is correct and indeed was used throughout post Second World War property boom periods. The weakness in approach and any errors in estimates were compensated for by property values increasing at a far greater rate than building costs, so developers could not avoid making high profits. Again, it was mainly the property crash of the early 1970s which made developers aware of the inherent weakness and the need to consider the cash flow throughout the development more carefully. In the days of log tables and slide rules, if a more sophisticated technique had been tried, the site would have been developed before the valuation completed!

Initially, an assumption was made that development would start immediately on purchase of the site which is clearly wrong; detailed planning permission is unlikely to have been obtained before purchase, nor detailed plans prepared. Finance details will need to be settled and contractors appointed, so there will be a 'lead-in' time between site acquisition and commencement of building work, during which, of course, the cost of purchase must be funded.

The project funding is known as the 'short-term' finance as distinct from the 'long-term' finance which is that used to purchase an investment. Project funding was considered to be borrowed at a uniform rate throughout the development period, known as 'straight line' borrowing, and therefore the mean amount was deducted. In practice this is not the case, as most of the building cost is incurred in the second half of the building period when more expensive materials and labour are used in the fitting out and provision of services. These total costs are represented by the so-called 'S curve', and by using an average cost an over-allowance for finance will result, thus reducing the amount available for site purchase. Another simplification of the method is that borrowing will not be at simple annual rate but more likely compounded on a period-by-period basis, monthly or quarterly. As explained earlier in the book, 3% paid quarterly is $(1.03)^4$, giving 12.55% not 12%, and thus will have a large effect particularly on interest accruing for the site. Further, retention sums will be held with part being released on completion and the remainder after a period following completion, usually six months, when minor defects might appear which require remedy.

In addition to assuming development begins immediately on purchase, the approach assumes that disposal on sale will occur on completion. In boom times this was happily so, but developers know now, to their cost, that this is not often the case. In commercial development schemes, developers seek to 'pre-let' the project, that is, to find a prospective tenant before the project is commenced. As well as reducing the developer's risk, this also reduces the perceived risk to the finance house, so providing more favourable finance terms. Unfortunately this is not always possible, especially in times of recession, the result being that the completed project remains unlet or unsold for a long period during which funding will still be required, and this must be allowed for in the appraisal.

An obvious way of reducing the funding problem is to phase the development so that cash inflow can be generated. In residential schemes this is fairly straightforward. Using example 13.1, the first house could be completed, say, after 9 months and sold, with the remainder being completed and sold over a further 3 months. Such well-laid plans rapidly founder in times of economic difficulties, with high bank base rates increasing mortgage borrowing, adverse changes in tax relief and credit restrictions. The construction industry is usually the first to suffer in such times. It was to reduce funding unsold houses that timber framed house building found favour with residential developers; houses could be erected rapidly after the purchaser had exchanged contracts. This met with reasonable success until the notorious television report exposing defects suffered by this form of construction. The sensational reporting implied that conventional houses suffer no construction defects.

In the past, commercial development schemes did not readily allow for phasing. Tenants do not welcome occupying premises with construction continuing around them; but business and retail parks and industrial estates lend themselves to phasing, thereby considerably reducing the funding requirements as well as the risk to the developer which increases the longer a scheme takes to complete.

On a modest scheme like that used in example 13.1, none of these errors and omissions are likely to be of great consequence. Development response to increases in demand for particular types of property must be relatively slow and all manner of national or international crises can occur which will put a project in jeopardy. However, as explained in chapter 3, by giving careful and detailed consideration to the cash flow generated by a development project, the risk will be reduced. As log tables and slide rules have been replaced by computers, a cash flow model for a scheme can be readily accommodated, either using a spreadsheet or commercial software (see chapter 14), and the sensitivity of a scheme to changes in borrowing rates or constructional delays assessed.

Applying a cash flow technique to example 13.1 with an assumed schedule of payments to the architect and contractor and disposal of one house a month for the last four months of the year is shown in table 13.1. It can be seen from this table that a positive balance of £81,056 is obtained after deducting the developer's profit. It will also be seen that a positive balance was achieved by the end of Month 11 and it has been assumed this will be invested at the borrowing rate until the completion of the scheme. If this were not the case, then obviously a lower final balance would be achieved. As in the simple residual valuation, the final balance will be the total cost of acquiring the site together with the fees and finance cost as before.

From the summary it can be seen that by incorporating a more realistic cash flow, incorporating projected sales and investing the credit balance, the amount allowed for funding has been reduced from £20,570, in the conventional method, to £8,944, the result being that a much higher figure can be offered for the site.

Table 13.2 includes the cost of site acquisition in the cash flow, the result being a nil balance showing that all the costs will be covered by sale of the houses and the expected developer's profit achieved. This is confirmed in the summary, where the total costs including site acquisition and developer's profit equal the net revenue from sales.

If a slightly more realistic scenario is taken, say building work does not commence until one month after buying the site, the houses still take twelve months to complete but do not come on stream until the tenth month, and the last one is not sold until one month after completion. The purchase price will again be affected unless the developer is prepared to accept a reduced profit. Table 13.3 sets out the cash flow, and the summary shows that finance is increased and the site price has fallen to £62,721.

Table 13.1 DEVELOPMENT STATEMENT   Project: Residential Development

Annual borrowing rate % 17
Periods per annum 12
Periods borrowing rate 0.01317

Period number	1	2	3	4	5	6	7	8	9	10	11	12
Expenditure												
Site: Cost												
Fees												
Contractor: cost	10,000	12,500	15,500	20,000	20,000	22,000	22,000	22,000	21,000	20,500	18,500	16,000
Fees: Architect	11,000			4,000				4,000				3,000
Developers required profit												60,000
Balance b.f.		21,277	34,221	50,376	75,356	96,612	120,174	144,046	172,285	96,540	19,291	−61,002
Total monthly expenditure	21,000	33,777	49,721	74,376	95,356	118,612	142,174	170,046	193,285	117,040	37,791	17,998
Income												
Sales									100,000	100,000	100,000	100,000
less Agent's fees @ 2%									2,000	2,000	2,000	2,000
Total Net Income	0	0	0	0	0	0	0	0	98,000	98,000	98,000	98,000
Outstanding balance	−21,000	−33,777	−49,721	−74,376	−95,356	118,612	−142,174	−170,046	−95,285	−19,040	60,209	80,002
Interest on balance	−277	−445	−655	−980	−1,256	−1,562	−1,872	−2,239	−1,255	−251	793	1,054
Cumulative balance c.f.	−21,277	−34,221	−50,376	−75,356	−96,612	−120,174	−144,046	−172,285	−96,540	−19,291	61,002	81,056

Summary

Sales:	£400,000	
less Agent's fees:	£ 8,000	
		£392,000
Total income:		
Construction	£220,000	
Architect fees	£22,000	
Total interest	£8,944	
Developer's profit	£60,000	
Total Costs		£310,944
Balance available for land		£81,056
PV £1@ 17% for 1 yr		0.855
		£69,278
Total acquisition cost		£69,278
Less Fees @ 0.03		£2,018
Site price		£67,260

Table 13.2 DEVELOPMENT STATEMENT Project: Residential Development

Annual borrowing rate % 17
Periods per annum 12
Periods borrowing rate 0.01317

Period number	1	2	3	4	5	6	7	8	9	10	11	12
Expenditure												
Site: Cost	67,260											
Fees	2,018											
Contractor: cost	10,000	12,500	15,500	20,000	20,000	22,000	22,000	22,000	21,000	20,500	18,500	16,000
Fees: Architect	11,000			4,000				4,000				3,000
Developer's required profit												60,000
Balance b.f.		91,467	105,336	122,427	148,356	170,573	195,109	219,968	249,208	174,476	98,253	19,000
Total monthly expenditure	90,278	103,967	120,836	146,427	168,356	192,573	217,109	245,968	270,208	194,976	116,753	98,000
Income												
Sales									100,000	100,000	100,000	100,000
less Agent's fees @ 2%									2,000	2,000	2,000	2,000
Total Net Income	0	0	0	0	0	0	0	0	98,000	98,000	98,000	98,000
Outstanding balance	−90,278	−103,967	−120,836	−146,427	−168,356	192,573	−217,109	−245,968	−172,208	−96,976	−18,753	0
Interest on balance	−1,189	−1,369	−1,591	−1,928	−2,217	−2,536	−2,859	−3,239	−2,268	−1,277	−247	0
Cumulative balance c.f.	−91,467	−105,336	−122,427	−148,356	−170,573	−195,109	−219,968	−249,208	−174,476	−98,253	−19,000	0

Summary
Sales:	£400,000
less Agent's fees:	£8,000
Total income:	£392,000
Site acquisition	£69,278
Construction	£220,000
Architect fees	£22,000
Total interest	£20,722
Developer's profit	£60,000
Total Costs	£392,000

Table 13.4 also confirms the nil balance when site acquisition costs are included in the cash flow.

Now let us look at a slightly more involved example.

Example 13.2

An office development has been proposed. The office block will have a gross floor area of 1,100 square metres and the net lettable floor area will be 80 per cent of gross. A rental yield of 8 per cent is expected to be obtained on a net rental value of £320 per square metre. Construction is planned to commence 6 months after the site is acquired and will take 15 months to complete. The premises will be let and sold as an investment 6 months after completion. Funding can be obtained at an annual rate of 17%.

A conventional valuation could be in the form set out in Table 13.5. The net developed value is based on the capitalised net rent (based on the net floor area) less the fees incurred in disposal. The building costs will be estimated on the gross floor area, the architect and associated design fees being taken at 13 per cent of the costs; a contingency allowance of 5 per cent is allowed for both the costs and the fees. Finance is taken for half the construction period, as before, followed by six months during which finance will be paid on the total cost, that is, including the building finance. The site purchase amount will have to be financed from the date of purchase and therefore the final sum is discounted for the total period of 27 months for the project. A resultant amount of £1,110,326 is available for purchase of the site.

A cash flow approach is set out in table 13.6. In this case, interest is to be paid at the end of each quarter, local authority fees and part of the design fees being paid in the first quarter with construction commencing in the third quarter. It is usual for a retention to be held by the developer, part being released on completion and the remainder after a period, generally six months. This retention allows for any minor defects to be remedied. Had the offices been let before being sold as an investment, the rent received would have been entered as income with a corresponding reduction in borrowing. On this flow basis, an offer of £1,180,348 could be made for the site.

The two treatments of this simple example illustrate that the basis of the traditional residual valuation used for development purposes remains unchanged, namely the deduction of development costs from the developed value. The cash flow approach gives a much more accurate valuation by requiring the valuer to give detailed consideration to all the cost elements likely to arise during the project. Computer models do not

Table 13.3 DEVELOPMENT STATEMENT — Project: Residential Development

Annual borrowing rate %	17
Periods per annum	12
Period borrowing rate	0.01317

Period number	1	2	3	4	5	6	7	8	9	10	11	12	13	14
Expenditure														
Site: Cost														
Fees														
Contractor: cost		10,000	12,500	15,500	20,000	20,000	22,000	22,000	22,000	21,000	20,500	18,500	16,000	
Fees: Architect		11,000			4,000				4,000				3,000	
Developer's required profit														60,000
Balance b.f.		0	21,277	34,221	50,376	75,356	96,612	120,174	144,046	172,285	195,831	119,889	40,921	−38,580
Total monthly expenditure	0	21,000	33,777	49,721	74,376	95,356	118,612	142,174	170,046	193,285	216,331	138,389	59,921	21,420
Income														
Sales											100,000	100,000	100,000	100,000
less Agent's fees @											2,000	2,000	2,000	2,000
Total Net Income	0	0	0	0	0	0	0	0	0	0	98,000	98,000	98,000	98,000
Outstanding balance	0	−21,000	−33,777	−49,721	−74,376	−95,356	−118,612	−142,174	−170,046	−193,285	−118,331	−40,389	38,079	76,580
Interest on balance	0	−277	−445	−655	−980	−1,256	−1,562	−1,872	−2,239	−2,545	−1,558	−532	501	1,009
Cumulative balance c.f.	0	−21,277	−34,221	−50,376	−75,356	−96,612	−120,174	−144,046	−172,285	−195,831	−119,889	−40,921	38,580	77,589

Summary

Sales:	£400,000	
less Agent's fees:	£8,000	
Total income:		£392,000
Construction	£220,000	
Architect fees	£22,000	
Total interest	£12,411	
Developer's profit	£60,000	
Total Costs		£314,411

Balance available for land £77,589
PV £1 @ 0.01317   14 periods   0.8326
Total acquisition cost £64,602
less: Fees at   0.03   £1,938
Site price   £62,721

Table 13.4 DEVELOPMENT STATEMENT   Project: Residential Development

Annual borrowing rate %	17
Periods per annum	12
Period borrowing rate	0.01317

Period number	1	2	3	4	5	6	7	8	9	10	11	12	13	14
Expenditure														
Site: Cost	62.721													
Fees	1.882													
Contractor: cost		10,000	12.500	15.500	20,000	20,000	22,000	22,000	21,000	20,500	18,500	16,000		
Fees: Architect		11,000			4,000				4,000				3.000	
Developer's required profit														60,000
Balance b.f.		65.454	87.592	101.411	118.450	144.326	166.490	190.973	215.777	244.962	269.464	194.492	116.507	38.001
Total monthly expenditure	64.603	86.454	100.092	116.911	142.450	164.326	188.490	212.973	241.777	265.962	289.964	212.992	135.507	98.001
Income														
Sales									0	0	100,000	100,000	100,000	100,000
less Agent's fees @ 2%									0	0	2,000	2,000	2,000	2,000
Total Net Income	0	0	0	0	0	0	0	0	0	0	98,000	98,000	98,000	98,000
Outstanding balance	−64.603	−86.454	−100.092	−116.911	−142.450	−164.326	−188.490	−212.973	−241.777	−265.962	−191.964	−114.992	37.507	−1
Interest on balance	−851	−1.139	−1.318	−1.540	−1.876	−2.164	−2.482	−2.805	−3.184	−3.503	−2.528	−1.514	−494	−0
Cumulative balance c.f.	−65.454	−87.592	−101.411	−118.450	−144.326	−166.490	−190.973	−215.777	−244.962	−269.464	−194.492	−116.507	38.001	−1

Summary		
Sales:	£400,000	
less Agent's fees:	£8,000	
Total income:		£392,000
Site acquisition	£64.603	
Construction	£220,000	
Architect fees	£22,000	
Total interest	£25,398	
Developer's profit	£60,000	
Total Costs		£392.001

Table 13.5

Gross floor area	1,100 m^2		
Net floor area	880 m^2		
Net income	880 m^2 @ £320/m^2	£281,600	
YP in perp. @ 8%		12.5	
Gross development value		£3,520,000	
Less sale costs @ 4%		140,800	
Net developed value			£3,379,200

Development costs

Building costs	1,100 m^2 @ £625/m^2	687,500	
Fees:			
Architect etc.	13.00%	89,375	
Local authority	2.5%	17,188	
Contingencies	5.00%	39,703	
Total			833,766
Finance costs			
Construction costs	833,766		
7.5 months @ 17%	0.1031		85,961
Letting time			
Accrued amount	919,727		
6 months @ 17%	0.0817		75,142
Letting cost			
Agent 10% of rent	28,160		
Legal 2%	5,632		33,792
Developer's profit			
20% Gross development value			704,000
Total development costs			1,732,661
Amount for site on completion			1,646,539
PV £1 for 2.25 years @ 17%			0.702
Amount for site acquisition			1,155,870
Less acquisition fees @ 4%			46,236
Amount for site			1,109,634
Estimated capital value of site			£1,110,000

Note: Quarterly rate used.

Table 13.6

Period number	1	2	3	4	5	6	7	8	9
Expenditure									
Site: Cost	30,000								
Fees	17,188								
Contractor: cost			68,750	120,312	144,375	171,875	182,187		
contingency			3,438	6,016	7,219	8,594	9,109		
less: retention			−3,609	−6,316	−7,580	−9,023	−9,565		
release: retention								18,047	18,047
Fees: Architect			11,000	11,000	11,000	11,000	11,000		4,375
Local authority									
Developer's required profit 0.12									704,000
Letting fees									33,792
Balance b.f.		49,077	51,042	135,849	277,543	449,873	657,631	884,404	938,577
Total monthly expenditure	47,188	49,077	130,620	266,860	432,557	632,318	850,363	902,451	1,698,791
Income									
Sale									3,520,000
less Agent's fees @ 0.04									140,800
Total Net Income	0	0	0	0	0	0	0	0	3,379,200
Outstanding balance	−47,188	−49,077	−130,620	−266,860	−432,557	−632,318	−850,363	−902,451	1,680,409
Interest on balance	−1,889	−1,965	−5,229	−10,683	−17,316	−25,313	−34,041	−36,126	67,269
Cumulative balance c.f.	−49,077	−51,042	−135,849	−277,543	−449,873	−657,631	−884,404	−938,577	1,747,678

Balance at end of project   £1,747,678   9 quarters
PV £1 @ 0.04003/quarter   0.702
Present amount for site   £1,227,562
Acquisition fees   4%   £47,214
Site value   £1,180,348

Note: Quarterly rate used.

Table 13.7 Viability Statement

Period number	1	2	3	4	5	6	7	8	9
Expenditure									
Site: Cost	1,180,348								
Fees	47,214								
Contractor: cost			68,750	120,312	144,375	171,875	182,187		
contingency			3,438	6,016	7,219	8,594	9,109		
less: retention			−3,609	−6,316	−7,580	−9,023	−9,565		
release: retention								18,047	18,047
Fees: Architect	30,000		11,000	11,000	11,000	11,000	11,000		4,375
Local authority	17,188								
Letting fees (0.12)									33,791
Balance b.f.		1,325,780	1,378,853	1,516,814	1,713,790	1,943,615	2,211,170	2,500,133	2,618,987
Total monthly expenditure	1,274,750	1,325,780	1,458,431	1,647,825	1,868,804	2,126,061	2,403,902	2,518,180	2,675,200
Income									
Sale									3,520,000
less Agent's fees @ 4%									140,800
Total Net Income	0	0	0	0	0	0	0	0	3,379,200
Outstanding balance	−1,274,750	−1,325,780	−1,458,431	−1,647,825	£1,868,804	−2,126,061	2,403,902	−2,518,180	704,000
Interest on balance	−51,030	−53,073	−58,383	−65,965	−74,811	−85,109	−96,232	−100,806	
Cumulative balance c.f.	−1,325,780	−1,378,853	−1,516,814	−1,713,790	−1,943,615	−2,211,170	−2,500,133	−2,618,987	
Balance Developer's Profit	£704,000								

Table 13.8 Viability Statement

Period number	1	2	3	4	5	6	7	8	9
Expenditure									
Site: Cost	1,200,000								
Fees	48,000								
Contractor: cost			68,750	120,312	144,375	171,875	182,187		
contingency			3,438	6,016	7,219	8,594	9,109		
less: retention			−3,609	−6,316	−7,580	−9,023	−9,565		
release: retention								18,047	18,047
Fees: Architect	30,000		11,000	11,000	11,000	11,000	11,000		4,375
Local authority 0.12	17,188								
Letting fees									33,792
Balance b.f.		1,347,036	1,400,960	1,539,806	1,737,703	1,968,485	2,237,036	2,527,034	2,646,964
Total monthly expenditure	1,295,188	1,347,036	1,480,538	1,670,817	1,892,717	2,150,931	2,429,767	2,545,081	2,703,178
Income									
Sale									3,520,000
less Agent's fees @ 4%									140,800
Total Net Income	0	0	0	0	0	0	0	0	3,379,200
Outstanding balance	−1,295,188	−1,347,036	−1,480,538	−1,670,817	−1,892,717	−2,150,931	−2,429,767	−2,545,081	676,022
Interest on balance	−51,848	−53,924	−59,268	−66,885	−75,768	−86,105	−97,267	−101,883	
Cumulative balance c.f.	−1,347,036	−1,400,960	−1,539,806	−1,737,703	−1,968,485	−2,237,036	−2,527,034	−2,646,964	

Balance Developer's Profit   £676,022

Return on Developed Value   20.01%

Return on Total Costs   25.01%

Summary

Sales:	£3,520,000	
less Agent's fees:	£140,800	
Total income:		£3,379,200
Site cost	£1,200,000	
Site fees	£48,000	
Construction	£721,875	
Architect fees	£89,375	
Local authority	£17,188	
Total interest	£592,948	
Letting fees	£33,792	
Total Costs		£2,703,178
Balance available for profit		£676,022

provide a magical solution, they only enable the otherwise tedious and repetitive calculations involved in a manual calculation to be avoided, and also facilitate financial monitoring of a project should any of the variables – costs, incomes, interest rates and time schedules – change.

Frequently the purchase price of the site is known, in which case the developer will need to know the profit to be made from a project. In this circumstance, the acquisition cost is included as a development expense in the residual valuation and then the resulting 'residue' is the amount of profit generated. Table 13.7 shows that the period cash flow approach can be used in the same way. Using example 13.2 and inserting the site costs as a cash outflow, the developer's expected profit of £704,000 will be achieved.

Where the amount for the site purchase is known, then the traditional method can be modified so that land acquisition is included as a development cost, together with the borrowing finance for it. The residue would thus indicate the developer's profit which would be made. Similarly, a cash flow viability statement can be prepared on the same lines. In the last example, should the site have to be purchased for £120,000, then the cash flow will show a reduced profit to £676,022, if all other costs remain unaltered. Table 13.8 shows the viability statement for these circumstances with the profit expressed as a return on the developed value and the total costs.

Viability statements are invaluable for monitoring a development project; changes in interest rates, delays in construction programme and variations in costs and sales forecasts can be readily inserted to project the resulting profit level.

There is no doubt that the traditional residual valuation still has its use, especially where a quick appraisal is required, but in the present competitive market where the dividing line between success and failure is so fine close and detailed consideration of the cash flow is of prime importance.

14 Computer Models and the Use of Spreadsheets

There can be little doubt that the surveying profession in general, and perhaps general practice in particular, has been reluctant, to say the least, to introduce the use of computers. Information technology, as the use of computers is now called, has been quite widely used in commerce and industry for many years, but until relatively recently the equipment required was huge and could only be operated by specialist personnel who surrounded their techniques with a range of mysterious jargon, an essential element of any profession! The more recent and rapid development of miniaturisation has enabled equipment to be available not only for desk-top but also lap-top use, and for some time now professional journals regularly report on the increasing amount of software packages produced for various aspects of surveying practice which does not need any specialist knowledge to operate. Nevertheless, much of this specialist software is designed for the widest market and therefore after purchase, at quite a high price, a surveyor might easily find it does not meet his specific needs; it is therefore left unused – confirming the view that it was not needed in the first place. This chapter is intended to explain that it is possible, without highly specialised knowledge, for surveyors to produce software to meet their own needs for operation on a relatively inexpensive personal computer.

COMPUTER SOFTWARE

This piece of computer terminology is now generally well understood to mean the programs which can be used on the computer machines, known as the 'hardware'. A relatively few enthusiastic practising surveyors have attempted to write their own programs, but it is a specialist skill and very time-consuming to test and 'debug' the work completely so as to produce a reliable product. Still fewer surveyors have managed to achieve this, and various surveying programs are now commercially available. This type of software is known as 'application specific', that is, a program for a single purpose such as project appraisal or residual valuation.

What is still not so widely appreciated is that there is another category of software known as 'stand-alone' programs which can be used for a number of different purposes, each 'customised' to carry out one or more specific tasks, yet requiring no special program writing skill. An electronic 'spreadsheet' is one such package.

Commercial spreadsheets were first introduced in 1979, but now there are something approaching one hundred available on the market, offering an enormous range of facilities as reflected in the price of each one. Spreadsheets have several advantages over specific programs: they are relatively cheap, offer greater flexibility for adaptation for different applications, have an ability to undertake a wide range of tasks, and provide the possibility of integration with other programs such as word processing, databases and graphics. The preparation of a calculation 'model' to perform these tasks can be undertaken relatively easily because no knowledge of formal program-writing is necessary.

A spreadsheet is a problem-solving tool capable of removing the tedium of carrying out a series of repetitive calculations and allowing the exploration of the effect that a change in one variable factor has on other related factors – for example, the change in short-term finance rate in a residual valuation. Spreadsheets are 'alphanumeric' which means that text as well as numbers can be incorporated in the program; in addition, word processing and graphics facilities enable calculations with diagrams to be incorporated into documents, such as accounting statements or valuation reports.

STRUCTURE OF A SPREADSHEET

Essentially, a spreadsheet is the equivalent of a sheet of paper divided into a grid of rows and columns. In a computer, it can be considered as an electronic grid. Depending on the program, the rows and columns are either numbered or lettered. Each box formed by the grid is known as a 'cell' and will have a unique reference from the column and row in which it is located. Not only can data, either numeric or text, be placed in a cell, but also formulae can be inserted which define the contents of one cell in terms of another. For example, if the number 3 is inserted in cell row 1 column A, and number 4 in cell row 1 column B, a formula multiplying the contents of these two cells could be inserted in cell row 1 column C; the result, 12, would instantly appear in that cell:

Column

		A	B	C	D	E	F	G
Row	1	3	4	12				
Row	2							
Row	3							

It is possible for any data contained in a cell to be overwritten; thus by changing the number to 5 in cell row 1 column A would immediately give the result as 20 in cell 1 column 4:

Column

		A	B	C	D	E	F	G
Row	1	5	4	20				
Row	2							
Row	3							

The size of the grid will depend on the spreadsheet program but can be considerable, enabling quite extensive and complex calculations to be undertaken. Where calculations such as a residual valuation or a viability statement will follow a structured format, 'templates' can be set up in the program; all that then needs to be done is for the relevant data to be inserted in the appropriate cells and the required result is immediately obtained. Though data can be overwritten in any cell, it is possible to 'lock' cells containing essential formulae in the program, thereby preventing any accidental alteration to the structure of the program.

Figure 14.1 illustrates a spreadsheet program written for the simple residual valuation examples used in chapter 13. The row and column numbers are shown but these would be omitted for a print to be produced for inclusion in, say, a valuation report. The template has been formed so that data, such as floor areas and building costs, can be inserted at the beginning of the program, the calculation formulae being placed in the lower section of the spreadsheet. Simply by inserting the data relevant to the development project being appraised, the valuation is immediately produced. The reader will note that there are some differences between the figures produced on the spreadsheet and those used in the example; this is because the spreadsheet is capable of far greater accuracy, for though a figure may be rounded to the nearest three decimal places in the print-out, it will in practice be used as though it were to seven or more

	1	2	3	4	5	6	7	8
1	RESIDUAL VALUATION							
2								
3	Office building							
4	Gross floor area	1100/sq.m.			Pre-contract time		6 months	
5	Net/gross area	80%			Construction cost		625/sq.m	
6	Sale yield	8%			Contingencies		5%	
7	Short term finance	17%			Retention:		5%	
8	Rent	£320/sq.m.			Release on completion		0%	
9	Development time	1.25 years			6 months after ditto		0%	
10					Disposal after ditto		6 months	
11	--							
12								
13	Net income			£281,600				
14	YP perp.		8	12.500				
15	Gross development value				3,520,000			
16	*Less* sale costs @	0.04			140,800			
17	Net development value					£3,379,200		
18	---							
19	Building costs							
20	Building			687,500				
21	Fees:							
22	Architect etc. % 13			89,375				
23	Local authority % 2.5			17,188				
24	Contingencies @ % 5			39,703				
25	Total				833,766			
26								
27	Finance costs							
28	Construction			£833,766				
29	0.625	years @	0.17	0.1031				
30					£85,964			
31	Letting time							
32	Amount			919,730				
33	6 months @ 0.17			0.0817	75,110			
34								
35	Letting Costs							
36	Agent % of rent 10			£28,160				
37	Legal ditto 2			5,632	£33,792			
38								
39	Developer's profit							
40	20% Development Value			£704,000				
41								
42	Total development costs				£1,732,632			
43	Amount for site on completion				£1,646,568			
44	PV £1 @ 2.25 years @ % 17				0.702			
45	Amount for site acquisition				1,156,542			
46	*Less* acquisition fees @ 4%				£46,262			
47	PRICE FOR SITE					£1,110,281		

Figure 14.1

places which can have a considerable effect when dealing with amounts running to millions of pounds.

'WHAT IF?' CALCULATIONS

It is well known that a relatively minor change in one of the variables in a residual valuation, such as a 1 per cent change in the capitalisation rate, can produce a considerably greater change in the resulting land value. Unfortunately such changes are frequently experienced during the course of a development project and can seriously affect the viability of the scheme, as witnessed by the Stock Market crash in 1987 and the more recent increases in short-term finance rates. Appraisers therefore need to pose questions such as 'what if the interest changes?' and 'what if unit building costs increase?'. Formerly, it would have been necessary to undertake a series of repetitive manual calculations, changing the data each time to produce answers to these questions. It can readily be seen that spreadsheets easily allow such data changes to be made, instantly producing answers to such 'what if?' problems. Figure 14.2 illustrates this by changing some of the data.

EQUATED YIELD

A further illustration of how the spreadsheet can be structured is shown in figure 14.3. This is a simple example of an equated yield application. At the top of the sheet is the space for the required data, at the bottom is the section in which the relevant formulae are produced. It will be noted that these are as in valuation tables. The calculations in the main structure of the analysis make reference to these formulae, and as before, as the data is changed so the results in the formulae section will alter, thereby adjusting the main calculations.

INTERNAL RATE OF RETURN

Most spreadsheets are programmed to carry out a number of set calculations by giving simple commands, such as summing columns or rows of figures and finding the mean of a set of data. In addition there are commands which have financial application, such as internal rate of return calculation. In figure 14.4 the data has been inserted at the top, with formulae incorporated, and the spreadsheet has been set to produce the income generated at each review. So, by commanding 'IRR', the internal rate of return is produced, in this case 21%.

	1	2	3	4	5	6	7	8
1	RESIDUAL VALUATION							
2								
3	Office building							
4	Gross floor area		1100/sq.m.		Pre-contract time		6 months	
5	Net/gross area		80%		Construction cost		600/sq.m	
6	Sale yield		8%		Contingencies		5%	
7	Short term finance		18%		Retention:		5%	
8	Rent		£330/sq.m.		Release on completion		0%	
9	Development time		1.5 years		6 months after ditto		0%	
10					Disposal after ditto		6 months	
11	---							
12								
13	Net income			£290,400				
14	YP perp.		8	12.500				
15	Gross development value				3,630,000			
16	*Less* sale costs @		0.04		145,200			
17	Net development value					£3,484,800		
18	--							
19	Building costs							
20	Building			660,000				
21	Fees:							
22	Architect etc. % 13			85,800				
23	Local authority % 2.5			16,500				
24	Contingencies @ % 5			38,115				
25	Total				800,415			
26								
27	Finance costs							
28	Construction			£800,415				
29	0.75 years @		0.18	0.1322				
30					£105,791			
31	Letting time							
32	Amount			906,206				
33	6 months @ 0.18			0.0863	78,186			
34								
35	Letting Costs							
36	Agent % of rent 10			£29,040				
37	Legal ditto 2			5,808	£34,848			
38								
39	Developer's profit							
40	20% Development Value				£726,000			
41								
42	Total development costs				£1,745,239			
43	Amount for site on completion				£1,739,561			
44	PV £1 @ 2.5 years @ % 18				0.661			
45	Amount for site acquisition				1,150,097			
46	*Less* acquisition fees @ 4%				£46,004			
47	PRICE FOR SITE						£1,104,093	

Figure 14.2

	1	2	3	4	5	6	7
1	EQUATED YIELD ANALYSIS						
2	--						
3							
4	INSERT DATA:			*			
5	Initial rent £	200		*			
6	Review periods	5 years		*			
7	All risks yield	12%					
8	Annual growth rate	6%		*			
9	--						
10							
11	Period	Years	Rent	PV £1 p.a.	PV £1	PV factor	PV sum
12				@ yield			
13	1	5	200	3.6048	1	3.6048	721
14	2	5	268	3.6048	0.5674	2.0454	547
15	3	5	358	3.6048	0.3220	1.1606	416
16	4	5	479	3.6048	0.1827	0.6586	316
17		Perpetuity	641	8.3333	0.1037	0.8639	554
18							
19							£2554
20							
21	Formulae						
22	Amt £1 for period:		1.3382				
23	Yield as a decimal:		0.12				
24	Rate as a decimal:		0.06				
25	Asf		0.1574				
26	PV £1 per annum		3.6048				

Figure 14.3

	1	2	3	4	5	6
1	INTERNAL RATE OF RETURN					
2						
3	Initial rent		24500 per annum net			
4	Review period		5 years			
5	Initial yield		5.5%		0.055	
6	Anticipated growth rate		6% per annum		0.06	
7	Amount of one pound p.a.		5 years		0.06	1.338
8	Present value	5 years	@	0.055	0.765	
9						
10						
11						
12	Purchase price					−445,455
13						
14	Income			24,500		
15		YP	5 years	@ 5.5	4.270	104,622
16						
17	First review					
18	Income			32,787		
19		YP	5 years	@ 5.5	4.270	
20		PV £1	5 years	@ 5.5	0.765	107,125
21						
22	Second review					
23	Income			42,851		
24		YP	5 years	@ 5.5	4.270	
25		PV £1	10 years	@ 5.5	0.585	107,125
26						
27	Third review					
28	Income			56,004		
29		YP	5 years	@ 5.5	4.270	
30		PV £1	15 years	@ 5.5	0.448	107,125
31						
32	Fourth review					
33	Income			73,195		
34		YP perp.	5.5%	def.	20	6.231	456,111
35						
36	IRR					0.210

Figure 14.4.

DATABASES

One of the traditional valuation 'arts' has been for the valuer to retain all his comparable data in his head, but just how accurate this was is open to question. Specific database programs can be purchased which enable a range of data to be stored and readily retrieved. The data can then be used for valuation and property purposes. Most spreadsheets include databases, and the data stored such as building costs, can easily be incorporated into valuation and appraisal work.

15 Financial Appraisal Techniques

This chapter extends the techniques of property investment appraisal into other areas. It looks first at capital appraisal techniques used in business, secondly at financial techniques used to analyse the performance of companies, and finally at the capital structures of companies.

CAPITAL APPRAISAL TECHNIQUES

Investment appraisal systems need a clear criterion on which to measure the proposals for investment in a project. The appraisal can only deal with money considerations, so items can then be quantified in cash terms. It cannot deal with qualitative assumptions, thus the criterion is based on a cash yardstick. The method used must also allow other alternative investment projects to be measured against one another.

In this section we look at the development of capital appraisal techniques in the business sector, for comparison with methods in the property sector. Just as in the property field, there is the contrast of traditional methods of property valuation with discounted cash flow approaches, and the development of capital appraisal techniques in business mirrors this. The traditional methods used in business, however, are more basic than those used in the property field. Property valuation methods take into account the concept of discounting income and costs in the future, which illustrates the time value of money in the sense that a £1 available today is worth more than a £1 in a year's time, even ignoring an inflation effect. This has been discussed earlier in the book but as a reminder, this is because if a £1 is immediately consumed, the benefit is obtained a year earlier or the £1 can be invested and earn interest over the year. In property valuation, the traditional Year's Purchase approach takes into account the time value of money, whereas traditional methods in business valuation ignore this. The more advanced approaches of discounted cash flow involving NPV and IRR are dealt with in other parts of this book, but so as to provide the reader with an overall picture and because these traditional business approaches are still widely used and give some useful information, they are outlined below. The two approaches discussed are the payback period method and the rate of return on investment method.

Payback Period Method

This method involves the calculation of the number of years that it takes to pay back the original investment in a project. The important criterion is the length of time: the shorter the period, the better the project.

Example 15.1

	PROJECTS		
	A	B	C
Investment	£10,000	£10,000	£10,000
Cash inflows (£)			
Year 1	1,000	7,000	7,000
2	9,000	2,000	0
3	2,000	3,000	3,000
4	0	0	7,000
Total cash inflows	12,000	12,000	17,000
Payback period	2 years	2 years	3 years
Ranking	1=	1=	3

Thus, on this basis, either project A or B could be chosen and there is no way to distinguish these in the analysis. Time in this analysis is used in a crude way, as it does not take into account the timing of the cash flows, for instance, high cash flows in the early years (in projects B and C compared with A) and also the cash flow after the payback period (project C). The advantage of such an approach is in its simplicity and its ability to recognise the time factor, although in a crude way, but no account is taken of the timing of the cash flows and of cash flows occurring after the payback cut-off point, and thus the approach ignores the overall profitability.

Rate of Return Method

This approach expresses a rate of profit as a percentage of the cost of an investment:

$$\frac{\text{Profit}}{\text{Cost}} \times 100\%$$

The cost figure is calculated by the capital employed in the project. A target return is set and if the profitability exceeds this figure then the project is acceptable. This is a replica of the basic traditional all risks yield in perpetuity.

$$\frac{\text{Net income}}{\text{Capital value}} \times 100\%$$

Note, however that the capital value in this context is the price paid or cost, and the yield is an initial yield. This appraisal is thus a form of valuation rather than an analysis of the investment.

In business finance, the calculation can be done on various bases, including the following:

- Profit can be before tax (PBIT = profit before interest and tax) or after tax.
- Profit figures can be for the first year, the maximum annual figure over the project life or the average figure over the project life. The last is usually considered the most suitable. Interest is the interest outstanding on debt raised by the company.
- The capital employed may be shown gross or as an average figure over the life of the asset, after deducting for depreciation each year.

Example 15.2

Investment	£8,000
Cash inflows (£)	
Year 1	4,000
2	6,000
3	4,000
4	2,000
Total cash inflow	16,000

Assuming there is no resale or scrap value to the investment, then the original £8,000 is lost at the end of the investment period and the depreciation on the investment is £8,000. Average profit is:

$$\frac{£16,000 - £8,000}{4 \text{ years}} = £2,000$$

Return on the investment before tax and any interest payment is:

$$\frac{£2,000}{£8,000} \times 100\% = 25\%$$

Depreciation in the calculation is taken as a straight line approach, allowing for an equal amount of the total depreciation per year. The advantage of this method is that it takes the same criterion related to profitability both for projects and the overall business. The choice of target rate could be the same rate as the firm sets for overall profitability. The choice of target rates has been discussed in chapter 4. The disadvantage of using this method is that it again ignores the time value of money. The use of a straight line approach to depreciation may not realistically reflect the timing of any negative cash flows.

In answer to the deficiencies of the traditional approaches in respect of their inability to take into account the time value of money, business has adopted the discounted cash flow techniques outlined earlier in the book.

Discounted Cash Flow Techniques

Discounted cash flow techniques are an important aid in the evaluation of investment proposals. The over-riding advantage of the DCF techniques is that they recognise the time value of money. You should remember that DCF analysis is only as accurate as the data put into the calculation. Where a rate is used in a DCF calculation, it is more useful as a yardstick than those approaches which use the traditional methods of payback period and return on investment. The evaluation of capital investment techniques has two difficulties. Firstly, costs and revenues arise at different times and this means that they are not directly comparable. This problem is handled by discounted cash flow. The second problem is that the future is uncertain and that forecasted cash flows may not arise as predicted. The reader should refer to chapter 11 on risk for more analysis of this problem.

The discounted cash flow approach appears to give a clear indication of the accept/reject decision for project appraisal, however this works well when there is only one project being considered in isolation. In reality the project will face competition in two forms. Firstly, there is the competition arising from the firm not having sufficient funds to accept all projects indicated as acceptable under the analysis. This is a problem of capital rationing and will be discussed later. The second problem is where two competing projects fulfil the same objective and only one is required. These problems have been analysed in the chapter on NPV and IRR, and show clearly that the NPV approach is preferred. The above analysis looked at individual projects but it may also be necessary to consider investment opportunities as part of a portfolio of investments; portfolio analysis is discussed in chapter 16.

We have looked at the major alternative investment techniques available in the commercial world and the choices that may be made between them. It is also necessary to look at the companies themselves, because such investigation will bring to light how capital appraisal techniques are used in companies and how cash flows are generated. There are rules governing the generation of the cash flows; these are related to the accounts of the company. In order to understand the financial affairs of a company, the appraiser must be aware of its financial standing and, if advising on investment in property assets, of the company's cost of capital. The cost of capital could affect the target discount rate used in discounted cash flow calculations (see chapter 3).

FINANCIAL ANALYSIS

Company Financial Statements

A company's financial statements are contained in the reports sent to their shareholders. The reports provide details of the operations of the company. It contains a Chairman's Review which looks at the preceding year and prospects for the future. There is also a Director's Report which comments on such matters as profits, dividends, fixed assets and finance, and includes the report of the auditors and a summary of the accounting policies of the company, which can be useful in the analysis of the financial position of the firm. Accounting policies are important in the property sector in respect of asset valuation, and there will be different bases according to whether a property company is an investment of a trading company. Attached to the report are the financial statements. These financial statements would be:

- The profit and loss account
- The balance sheet
- Notes to the accounts
- Current cost accounts
- A statement of source and applications of funds
- A statement of value added.

The balance sheet and the profit and loss account are the main statements of the financial situation of the company. The balance sheet would be for an individual or group of companies, but if there were a parent company then this may be included. The main accounts would be in accordance with historic cost conventions, but current cost accounts would attempt to take into account inflation in asset values.

The Balance Sheet

The balance sheet lists the balances of assets and liabilities as at the accounting date. As a result of the EEC's fourth directive on company accounts, balance sheets will now be in a standardised form. The sheets are built up from three categories of entry: assets, liabilities and shareholders' funds. Thus total assets are equal to the sum of shareholders' funds plus liabilities if one looks at the balance sheet from the point of view of the company; alternatively, from a shareholders' view, one can see that the difference between assets and liabilities is the shareholders' funds.

Liabilities	*Assets*
Shareholders' funds	Fixed assets
Long-term liabilities	Current assets
Short-term liabilities	

TOTAL LIABILITIES	=	TOTAL ASSETS

Summary

Business view: assets = shareholders' funds + liabilities.

Shareholders' view: assets − liabilities = shareholders' funds.

Fixed assets + Net current assets (current assets less current liabilities) = Capital employed (shareholders' funds + long-term liabilities).

(This is a modification of the business view, taking current liabilities to the asset side of the equation.)

Profit and Loss Account

While the balance sheet is a measure of the financial worth of the company at a particular moment in time, a profit and loss account covers a period of time, say for the year ending on the accounting date; it is the result of the year's activities. The profit is shown before and after tax. Profit attributable to minority interests arises from investment in other companies amounting to 50% or less of ownership, and these profits are not allowed to be consolidated in the sheet. The accounts also show the proportion of profit distributed and retained. To grow, a company will need to increase its assets. The balance sheet shows that assets = liabilities plus shareholders' funds, so that the ways to grow would be to increase liabilities (borrow more) or increase shareholders' funds. There are two ways of increasing the shareholders' funds: by issuing more shares or by ploughing back profits. Ploughing back profits is not necessarily the cheapest source of long-term funds for the company and it also restricts the payment of dividends.

Basic Accounting Concepts

The financial statements that are produced are based on accounting concepts. Four rules or concepts are observed in all published accounts, unless otherwise stated. These rules are:

- The going concern concept
- The accruals concept
- The consistency concept
- The prudence concept.

The going concern concept assumes that the business will be continuing its activities for the foreseeable future on a similar scale. Thus the values attaching to assets and liabilities in the Balance Sheet reflect going concern values. This concept is important in property asset valuation for accounts purposes.

The accruals concept states that it is vital in an assessment of profit and loss for the accounting period to compare costs and benefits accurately. It is important to assign costs and financial returns to the period incurred, which may not be the same time period when money costs are incurred or financial returns received. For instance, if a sale has legally taken place, whether or not cash has been received from the customer for the goods delivered, the transaction will be taken as a sale and included as part of the sales revenue appearing in the profit and loss account.

The consistency concept is necessary so that approaches to the formulation of the accounts remain the same, and so valid comparisons and analysis can be made against previous results and with other companies.

The prudence concept covers the attitudes of dealing with costs and revenues; it is the cautious way an accountant approaches the problem by considering losses in full (even if doubtful), but never including a profit unless it is certain. Based on the above concepts, the Companies Act makes it a legal requirement that a company's Balance Sheet should show a true and fair view.

Techniques for Analysis

The analysis of company accounts involves the initial consideration of three problems:

1. Is the company making a satisfactory profit?
2. Is the company short of cash or cash rich?
3. What should be the source of long-term funds?

These problems relate to profitability, liquidity and capital structure, and are as applicable to individual property projects as they are to property companies or any firm. The techniques applied are based on relationships between the elements in the financial statements (financial ratios) and rates of return (yields). The area of capital structure is a major one which also has parallels in the financial construction of property projects.

Profitability Measures

The key ratios used to analyse the profitability of an enterprise are:

1. Trading profit as a percentage of turnover.
2. Profit before interest and tax as a percentage of average capital employed.
3. Earnings per share, either basic (based on issued share capital) or fully diluted (based on authorised share capital, which is the total share capital that can be issued).
4. Dividend per share.
5. Number of times covered – that is, the number of times a dividend is covered by earnings. This is also a measure used by property managers to assess the security of a tenant by testing the number of times the rent is covered by the net profit of the tenant company.
6. Assets per share – the asset backing of shares based on the value of the net assets divided by the number of shares. There has been much discussion in this area, specifically in relation to the share price of property investment companies as one would expect the asset value per share to relate to the market price of the share. However, traditionally the market has discounted the net asset values of property investment companies historically by an average of approximately 20%. The discount is measured by (Isaac and Woodroffe, 1986):

$$\frac{\text{Share price} - \text{Net asset value per share}}{\text{Net asset value per share}} \times 100\%$$

Return on Investment

This is defined as:

$$\frac{\text{Profits}}{\text{Assets}} \times 100\%$$

Thus profit is looked at as a percentage of capital and this is further influenced by two other ratios comprising the profit margin (profit as a percentage of sales) and the rate of asset turnover (sales divided by assets).

$$\frac{\text{Profit}}{\text{Assets}} = \frac{\text{Profit}}{\text{Sales}} \times \frac{\text{Sales}}{\text{Assets}}$$

or

$$\text{Return on Capital} = \text{Profit Margin} \times \text{Turnover}$$

The return on capital will vary from one industry to another, but wider variations may be found in the profit margin and rates of turnover. For instance, a return of 20% could be achieved by a high profit margin and a low turnover (the corner shop) or low profit margin and high turnover (the supermarket piling the goods high and selling cheap).

A sector comparison would show that capital-intensive industries with long production cycles have a low rate of turnover but a high profit margin. From the key ratios above, a number of subsidiary ratios relating costs or assets to sales can be formulated. Depending on the use to which the ratio is put, the definitions of profit and assets will differ. Generally a wider view of company performance is taken:

$$\text{Return on Capital} = \frac{\text{Profit before Tax, Interest and Dividends}}{\text{Total Capital Employed}}$$

The comparison of profitability ratios enables firms within a sector to be compared against one another, and for the various sectors to be compared.

Liquidity and Cash Flows

As well as being profitable, it is also important that a company should be liquid. A profitable and fast expanding company may find that it has tied up its profits in fixed assets, stocks and debtors and that it has difficulty paying its debts as they fall due. There are two main ratios to examine the liquidity of a company: the liquidity ratio and the current ratio.

The liquidity ratio is also called the 'acid test ratio' because it is a most important test. It is the ratio of liquid assets to current liabilities and a 1:1 ratio means that a company has sufficient cash to pay its immediate debts. Liquid assets are defined as current assets, excluding stocks of goods which cannot be quickly turned into cash. In effect, liquid assets are debtors, cash and any short-term investments like bank deposits or Government securities. A company can survive with a liquid ratio of less than 1:1 if it has an unused bank overdraft facility.

The other test of a company's liquidity is the current ratio, which includes stocks and work in progress on the grounds that stocks eventually turn into debtors and then into cash itself. It is calculated by relating all current assets to current liabilities. A norm of 2:1 is generally regarded as being satisfactory, but this will depend on the particular sector.

Thus:

$$\text{Liquidity Ratio} = \text{Liquid Assets:Current Liabilities}$$

$$\text{Current Ratio} = \text{Current Assets:Current Liabilities}$$

CAPITAL STRUCTURE

The question of an optimal capital structure for a particular company is a question which has aroused much debate. The problem is the choice of the best mix of debt (loans, debentures) and equity (ordinary shares, reserves and retained profits). The following factors ought to be considered, but assessing the weight to be given to each one is a matter of judgement:

1. *Cost*
   The current and future costs of each potential source of capital should be estimated and compared. The costs of each source are not independent of one another. It is generally desirable to minimise the average overall cost of capital to the company.
2. *Risk*
   It is unwise to place a company in a position where it may be unable, if profits fall, to pay interest as it falls due or to meet redemptions. It is equally undesirable to be forced to cut or omit the ordinary dividend to shareholders.
3. *Control*
   Except where there is no alternative, a company should not make any issue of shares which would have the effect of removing or diluting control by the existing shareholders.

4. *Acceptability*

A company can only borrow if investors are willing to lend to it. Few listed companies can afford the luxury of a capital structure which is unacceptable to the main institutional investors. A company with readily mortgagable assets will find it easier to raise debt.

5. *Transferability*

Shares may be listed or unlisted. Many private companies have made issues to the public so as to obtain a listing on the Stock Exchange and improve the transferability of their shares.

Cost of Capital

A company cannot always choose the cheapest source of capital because of the need to pay attention to the factors indicated in the previous section. The costs of each potential source of capital should be estimated to reduce the average cost of capital. The costs of issuing capital need to take into account any tax benefits, for instance, the interest on loan stock or debentures can be reduced by the tax benefit as the interest is deductible for tax purposes. This would not be so for preference shares which would have the same rate before and after tax.

The cost of issue of ordinary shares is more difficult to calculate:

$$\text{Gross dividend yield} = \frac{\text{current dividend per ordinary share}}{\text{market price per share}} \times 100\% \times \frac{100}{75}$$

The multiplier 100/75 is to allow for the tax credit. The dividend yield of any company can be compared with dividend yields in general and with those of other companies in the same equity group. The dividend yield prior to the 1960s tended to be higher than the yield obtained on unredeemable Government stocks, because of the greater risk associated with equities. Since that time, the effects of inflation have caused a reverse yield gap in which the yield for equities has fallen below that of gilts as prices are bidded higher. This is because equities have an ability to protect the owner against inflation; they tend to be inflation-proof rather than inflation-prone as gilts are. Redeemable debentures and loans issued by companies would tend to have a higher yield than Government stock because they have a higher risk, but they are also inflation-prone as the returns are fixed. The dividend yield cannot be regarded as an adequate measure of the cost of equity capital as it does not take into account future change in the dividend stream and general changes in share price levels.

Two possible measures of the cost of equity capital are the earnings yield and the dividend yield plus a growth rate built in.

The earnings yield is:

$$\frac{\text{Earnings per ordinary share after tax}}{\text{Market price per ordinary share}} \times 100\%$$

but it is more usual to express this as a price: earnings ratio, that is:

$$\frac{\text{Market price per ordinary share}}{\text{Earnings per ordinary share after tax}}$$

The higher the *P/E* ratio (or alternatively the lower the earnings yield), the more the market thinks of the company and the cheaper the cost of equity capital. Earnings per share are calculated after the deduction of tax and preference dividends.

Dividend cover is also an important tool for analysis. Since the market is interested in future dividends it prefers to see current dividends reasonably well covered by current earnings; this is a form of guarantee that the dividend will be maintained in the future. The *Financial Times* measure of dividend cover is:

$$\frac{\text{Earnings per share on a maximum basis}}{\text{Ordinary dividend per share}}$$

Earnings per share on a maximum basis assumes that a company distributes all its profits and is liable to pay advance corporation tax on them.

An alternative approach to the cost of equity capital is to add a growth rate to the dividend yield. If one considers that a company's dividends will grow at the rate of, say, 8% then this is added to the gross dividend yield to give the total cost of equity capital.

A further approach to calculating the cost of equity capital is that developed by portfolio theory. This cost is estimated as:

$$R_f = \beta[E(R_m) - R_f]$$

where R_f is the return on a riskless security (such as a Treasury Bill). $E(R_m)$ is the expected return on all securities in the market and β (beta) is a measure of risk. These aspects were covered in more detail in chapter 11.

Application of the Cost of Capital to a Project

If a project has a return of 20% to equity capital, it can be refinanced at different levels of debt. The gearing effect is shown by increasing the level of debt, which increases the return to equity capital dramatically.

Example 15.3

Assume that Project return = 30% and debt capital costs = 15%. The project is financed by 50% equity and 50% debt.

The returns on the project are distributed as returns to the debt holders or to the equity holders on the basis of their holdings:

$$R_p = (0.5)\ R_e + (0.5)R_d$$

where R_p, R_d and R_e are the returns to the project, debt and equity capital respectively. Thus:

$$30\% = (0.5)R_e + (0.5)\ 15\%$$

$$R_e = \frac{30\% - 7.5\%}{0.5} = 45\%$$

The value of a project will not alter merely by the way it is financed, but this will affect the way the proceeds are distributed, and thus the gearing is affected. If the project is financed 20% equity and 80% debt then:

$$30\% = (0.2)\ R_e + (0.8)\ 15\%$$

$$R_e = \frac{30\% - 12\%}{0.2} = 90\%$$

The advantage of using debt is that besides the gearing effect on the return to equity, the interest on debt is tax deductible and the analysis can be further advanced by using the weighted cost of capital by calculating the returns to equity and debt and adjusting the debt return for tax relief. Thus a project may provide a valuable tax shield (see chapter 16).

REFERENCE

Isaac, D. and Woodroffe, N. (1986). 'Corporate Finance and Property Development Funding', Working Paper, Polytechnic of the South Bank, London.

16 New Directions

This chapter will look at a number of issues which extend the theory and examples in the rest of the book. It extends the analysis of risk in the single project by considering portfolio analysis. It extends the application of taxation and the cost of capital by looking at the adjusted present value method. Finally, it extends the application of the explicit discounted cash flow approach by considering depreciation in property appraisal.

PORTFOLIO ANALYSIS

Quantitative measures can be allocated to concepts of return and risk. We have seen this in operation in chapter 11. Returns are measured by expected cash flow returns but risks are measured by standard deviation (σ) and variance (σ^2) (note that σ is not risk, but a surrogate for risk).

RISK DIVERSIFICATION

Assume that an investor has two investment opportunities, A and B, and that these opportunities produce the following data:

		Opportunity A	Opportunity B
Return %	x	3 or 7	9 or 1
Probability of each return		0.5	0.5
Expected return	$\bar{x}$	5	5
Variance %	σ^2	4	16
Standard deviation %	σ	2	4

Variance = σ^2 and is the sum of the differences between the return and the expected returns squared and divided by the number of returns:

$$\sigma^2 = \frac{\Sigma \, (x - \bar{x})^2}{n}$$

For $A = \dfrac{(3-5)^2 + (7-5)^2}{2}$ For $B = \dfrac{(9-5)^2 + (1-5)^2}{2}$

$$\sigma^2 = 4 \qquad\qquad \sigma^2 = 16$$
$$\sigma = \sqrt{4} \qquad\qquad \sigma = \sqrt{16}$$
$$\sigma = 2 \qquad\qquad \sigma = 4$$

Both opportunities have the same expected return but differ in risk. *B* has a greater variance than *A* and is therefore more risky. Rational decision-makers faced with two projects of the same return will take one with less risk. If the investor invests in both, let us assume that the projects are inversely correlated. Assume the decision-maker invests $\frac{2}{3}$ of funds in *A* and $\frac{1}{3}$ in *B*.

The expected return on the portfolio is the weighted average of the returns on the individual opportunities, using the fraction of the funds in each as weights:

$$ER_p = \sum_{i=1}^{n} x_i \, (E_i)$$

where ER_p is the return on the portfolio, x_i is the proportion invested in opportunity i and E_i is the expected return on opportunity i.

$$ER_p = \tfrac{2}{3}(5) + \tfrac{1}{3}(5) = 5$$

The expected return is the same as if one had directly invested in *A* or *B*. However, the risk of the portfolio is reduced if *A* and *B* are inversely correlated. When *A* is a high return, then *B* is low and vice versa.

$$A \text{ high: } ER_p = \tfrac{2}{3}(7) + \tfrac{1}{3}(1) = 5$$
$$B \text{ high: } ER_p = \tfrac{2}{3}(3) + \tfrac{1}{3}(9) = 5$$

Risk of the portfolio is 0 ($\sigma = 0$).

Combining two risky opportunities, the decision-maker has achieved a risk-free return. The situation has arisen because the opportunities are inversely correlated (coefficient of correlation = -1) and the proportion of funds invested in each was determined on this basis.

The effect is technically called 'diversification' and is an example of the statement that risk can be diversified away. For a single opportunity, it is necessary to consider the expected return and variance; for two or more opportunities, it is necessary additionally to consider their interactive risk. This is covariance. Further analysis is outside the scope of this book and the reader is recommended to more academic texts (such as Brown, 1988).

TAXATION AND THE COST OF CAPITAL

Gerald Brown (1987) has considered the use of a Present Value method to bring together the financing and tax aspects of a project. Chapter 15 noted that there were gearing effects and tax considerations when financing with debt capital. Financing with debt creates a valuable tax shield; this is important in the property sector because property projects tend to support high levels of debt.

A project under this basis can be split into two parts as follows:

Project Value = value assuming wholly equity financed + value of the tax shield

This is called the Adjusted Present Value (APV) rule and for individual projects would be calculated from the following:

APV = Base case NPV + PV Tax shield

The analysis of the project splits into two parts. The first part analyses the net of tax incremental cash flows and capitalises them at a net of tax risk adjusted rate. The second part takes the interest payment on the debt and multiplies it by the corporate tax rate. This is then discounted back to its present value at a rate applicable to debt. So two cash flows are used at different rates to reflect the risks involved (see chapter 11 for a discussion of risk).

Example 16.1

A project costing £100m will generate a cash flow of £30m in perpetuity. The project will be financed 70% debt and 30% equity. The return to debt is 15%, the equity return required is 20% net of tax and the rate of corporation tax is 35%.

Equity cash flows:

$$\text{NPV of net of tax equity cash flows} = \frac{\text{net of tax cash flow}}{\text{yield}} - \text{cost}$$

$$\frac{£30m \times (1 - 0.35)}{0.20} - £100 = - £2.5m$$

Present value of the tax shield in perpetuity (PVT):

$$= \frac{\text{debt} \times \text{debt interest rate} \times \text{tax \%}}{\text{debt yield}}$$

$$= \frac{\text{£70m} \times 0.15 \times 0.35}{0.15} = \text{£24.5m}$$

Adjusted present value $= -\text{£2.5m} + \text{£24.5m} = \text{£22m}$.

This approach is useful in analysing the effect of capital structure and tax effects. In the example, the project produces a negative NPV on the basis of a wholly equity financed operation and would not be attractive to a wholly equity financed firm. However, if the firm pays tax then it may be profitable from the point of view of the tax shelter.

DEPRECIATION

Depreciation has been defined as "the measure of wearing out, consumption or other loss of value of a fixed asset whether arising from use, effluxion of time or obsolescence through technology or market changes." (Bowie, 1982). Accountants will charge depreciation to an asset and simply by looking at the purchase price and sale price or scrap value, they will write off the value over the life of the asset. Example 16.2 is a simple case of this.

Example 16.2

A car is purchased for £10,000. It is estimated that it will last 4 years before being resold for £2,000. The car can be written down using a straight line method (there are other approaches), thus:

Purchase price	£10,000	
less Resale price	£2,000	
Amount to be written off	£8,000	
Life of asset		4 years
Depreciation per year	£2,000	

A straight line method of course will not take into account the greater amount of depreciation in the earlier years. Depreciation can be divided into curable and incurable depreciation. Curable depreciation relates to maintenance, but incurable relates to obsolescence. Obsolescence can be further divided into internal obsolescence, such as the wearing out of a building (the technical changes which render space useless), and external obsolescence which relates to the decay of the environment, such as changes in the location of industry. Bowie (1982) suggests that by taking the potential life span of different properties one can estimate the true depreciated yield.

Example 16.3

Assume an industrial building has a 40 year life span. When the building is new, the land content is 20% value and the initial yield is 7.5% for each £100 invested.

	£
Total investment	100
less Land value	20
Building value	80

Depreciated over a 40 year life = £2 p.a. = 2% of £100 investment

Thus true depreciated yield = 7.5% − 2% = 5.5%.

Salway (1987) suggests that there are three methods of investment appraisal which can allow explicitly for an analysis of building depreciation:

1. Treat the built element as a leasehold interest.
2. Use a cost base approach.
3. Use an explicit DCF appraisal over the life of the building.

Salway uses the latter approach to develop a DCF appraisal over a limited time period which equates to the anticipated life of the building in its existing form. Allowance is made for the effects of depreciation in two ways. Firstly, the appraiser chooses a new-building growth rate and then specifies the percentage of the new-building rental value expected to be achieved at each successive rent review. Secondly, the terminal capital value is taken to be the estimated residual value of the property for refurbishment or redevelopment. This is based on present-day prices inflated over the time period at the new building growth rate. The DCF is used to provide a NPV given a discount rate and a projected net of depreciation growth rate, or a discount rate or net of depreciation growth rate given the other two variables. The terminal value is represented by the site value, the residual value on refurbishment or the investment value if relet. If there is uncertainty about the outcome then probability techniques can be used.

Example 16.4

The probability of the terminal outcome of a property asset is assessed as follows:

Outcome	Value	Probability
Site value	300,000	0.2
Residual value on refurbishment	400,000	0.5
Investment value, relet unimproved	450,000	0.3

Terminal value = $(300,000 \times 0.2) + (400,000 \times 0.5) + (450,000 \times 0.3) =$ £395,000.

CONCLUSION

The Royal Institution of Chartered Surveyors/Polytechnic of the South Bank report on 'Property Valuation Methods' was published in July 1986. It recommended, in general, the adoption of a number of the techniques discussed in this book (Trott, 1986). This book takes the analysis further and in general this book supports the adoption of an explicit discounted cash flow approach in property appraisal (see also Baum and Crosby, 1988). Successful developments in valuation theory have been based on cash flow approaches incorporating probability and decision-making techniques to allow for risk. Further developments considered in this book have included the incorporation of depreciation in the analysis. The asset base of the developer or investor has also been considered as opposed to a project-based traditional approach. The use of a financial outlook rather than a project-by-project approach is exemplified by the adoption of portfolio analysis in the appraisal of property assets.

REFERENCES

Baum, A. and Crosby, N. (1988). *Property Investment Appraisal*, Routledge and Keegan Paul, London.

Bowie, N. (1982). *Depreciation: Who hoodwinked whom?*, Estates Gazette, London, 1 May.

Brown, G. R. (1987). 'Analysing Property Developments', paper given at a conference on Property Development Appraisals, Cafe Royal, London.

Brown, G. R. (1988). *Portfolio Theory and Property Investment Analysis*, in A. R. MacLeary and N. Nanthakamaran (eds), *Property Investment Theory*, Spon, London.

Salway, F. (1987). 'Building Depreciation and Property Appraisal Techniques', *Journal of Valuation*, Volume 5, No. 5.

Trott, A. (ed.) (1986). 'Property Valuation Methods', Research Report, Royal Institution of Chartered Surveyors/Polytechnic of the South Bank, July.

Index